THE BEANS & PULSES
COOKBOOK

THE BEANS & PULSES COOKBOOK

Over 85 deliciously healthy and wholesome low-fat recipes for every meal and occasion, with more than 450 step-by-step stunning photographs

How to use beans, nuts, legumes and pulses to create enticing and nutritious dishes for improved health and an energized lifestyle

consultant editor: Simona Hill

southwater

This edition is published by Southwater, an imprint of
Anness Publishing Ltd, Hermes House, 88–89 Blackfriars Road
London SE1 8HA; tel. 020 7401 2077; fax 020 7633 9499

www.southwaterbooks.com; www.annesspublishing.com

If you like the images in this book and would like to investigate
using them for publishing, promotions or advertising, please visit
our website www.practicalpictures.com for more information.

UK agent: The Manning Partnership Ltd
tel. 01225 478444; fax 01225 478440
sales@manning-partnership.co.uk

UK distributor: Grantham Book Services Ltd
tel. 01476 541080; fax 01476 541061
orders@gbs.tbs-ltd.co.uk

North American agent/distributor: National Book Network
tel. 301 459 3366; fax 301 429 5746; www.nbnbooks.com

Australian agent/distributor: Pan Macmillan Australia
tel. 1300 135 113; fax 1300 135 103
customer.service@macmillan.com.au

New Zealand agent/distributor: David Bateman Ltd
tel. (09) 415 7664; fax (09) 415 8892

Publisher: Joanna Lorenz
Editorial Director: Helen Sudell
Editor: Simona Hill
Designer: Ian Sandom
Production Controller: Pedro Nelson

10 9 8 7 6 5 4 3 2 1

© Anness Publishing Ltd 2007

Previously published as part of a larger volume,
The Big Bean Cookbook

ETHICAL TRADING POLICY

Because of our ongoing ecological investment programme, you, as
our customer, can have the pleasure and reassurance of knowing
that a tree is being cultivated on your behalf to naturally replace
the materials used to make the book you are holding. For further
information about this scheme, go to
www.annesspublishing.com/trees

NOTES

Bracketed terms are intended for American readers.

For all recipes, quantities are given in both metric and imperial
measures and, where appropriate, in standard cups and spoons.
Follow one set of measures, but not a mixture, because they are
not interchangeable.

Standard spoon and cup measures are level. 1 tsp = 5ml,
1 tbsp = 15ml, 1 cup = 250ml/8fl oz.

Australian standard tablespoons are 20ml. Australian readers
should use 3 tsp in place of 1 tbsp for measuring small
quantities of gelatine, flour, salt, etc.

The nutritional analysis given for each recipe is calculated per
portion (i.e. serving or item), unless otherwise stated. If the
recipe gives a range, such as Serves 4–6, then the nutritional
analysis will be for the smaller portion size, i.e. 6 servings.
Measurements for sodium do not include salt added to taste.

CONTENTS

INTRODUCTION   6

   LEGUMES   8
   PULSES   10
   SPROUTED BEANS, AND
     LENTILS   16
   SOYA BEAN PRODUCTS   18

APPETIZERS AND SOUPS   22

SALADS AND SIDE DISHES   50

VEGETARIAN   66

POULTRY AND MEAT   92

FISH AND SHELLFISH   116

INDEX   127

INTRODUCTION

For thousands of years, pulses (encompassing peas, beans and lentils) have been staple foods for many civilizations. They are culturally and historically significant. The lentil, for example, is believed to be one of the first plants ever "farmed" by humanity. In fact, within some cultures the humble lentil almost reached mythical status – the Egyptians praised the lentil for its ability to enlighten the mind. In China, sprouted beans were used to treat a wide range of illnesses, from constipation to dropsy. In India, remains of green peas, red lentils and kesari beans have been found dating from 1800–2000BC.

Mung beans and urd beans have also been consumed on the subcontinent since ancient times. Written records from different periods of history confirm that pulses have been a major component of our diets. Early texts mention a number of pulses that are still farmed today, including chickpeas, cowpeas and pigeon peas. More recent introductions include jackbeans, lima, broad (fava) and kidney beans, which were introduced from South America.

VERSATILITY

What is truly remarkable about these staple ingredients is their versatility and how they have been transformed by civilizations throughout the world into a staggering range of foods. In India, which produces more pulses than any other country, there are at least 60 different kinds of dhal made from peas, beans and lentils. Pulses are also finely ground to make pancakes, flatbreads, poppadums and dosa.

Pulses and grains are experiencing a resurgence in popularity. They've become "upwardly mobile" – no longer seen as a poor man's food or that of the puritanical wholefood fanatic. With this

Above: Different varieties of lentils are available. Red lentils need no soaking and less cooking time than other types.

renewed interest, we've seen new, or more accurately previously unseen, varieties on many restaurant menus and in food shops.

HEALTH ATTRIBUTES

Pulses contain a high concentration of nutrients. They contain proportionately less carbohydrates yet more protein than grains. They are very low in fat, mostly the unsaturated kind, and are a good source of B vitamins, iron, magnesium and fibre. While dried beans lose most of their vitamin C content in the drying process, canned beans manage to retain half of their vitamin C and contain a higher percentage of calcium and vitamin E than dried. Soya beans are nutritionally superior to other pulses being richer in protein, iron and calcium. Pulses can be sprouted too, which greatly enhances their nutritional value.

Recently, scientists at University College, London, discovered that a diet rich in beans, nuts and cereals could be a way to help prevent cancer. They found that these foods contain a potent anti-cancer compound, which, researchers say, in the future may be possible to mimic in an anti-cancer drug.

Left: Burritos are a popular Mexican fast food. These wheat-flour tortillas are often filled with spicy bean mixtures.

Above: Chickpeas are one of the oldest crops farmed by man. Dried chickpeas need soaking before cooking but canned chickpeas are ready to use.

Right: Yellow split peas have a sweet and mild flavour. They are sold dried, and the pea is split into two.

STORAGE

One of the biggest advantages of many dried beans is that they have a long shelf life if kept in dry, cool airtight containers away from sunlight. However, it's best to eat dried beans as fresh as possible as they toughen with age and consequently take longer to cook.

Below: Puy lentils have a peppery flavour and hold their shape in cooking.

Modern canning methods mean that canned pulses are often more nutritious than fresh but are also more convenient. No pre-soaking or long cooking times are necessary, and since canned beans are softer in texture they only need heating through. Some argue, however, canned beans can't compete on flavour.

Below: Cannellini beans provide an excellent source of iron.

PULSES

A pulse is the collective term for the edible dried seeds of plants belonging to the Leguminosae, including beans, peas and lentils. There are around 13,000 species and the Leguminosae family is the second largest in the plant kingdom. Pulses sustain a large number of people in the world and are important economically. Surprisingly, the groundnut or peanut is also part of this family.

LEGUMES

LENTILS, PEAS AND PULSES PROVIDE THE COOK WITH A DIVERSE RANGE OF FLAVOURS AND TEXTURES. THEY HAVE LONG BEEN A STAPLE FOOD IN THE MIDDLE EAST, SOUTH AMERICA, INDIA AND THE MEDITERRANEAN, BUT THERE IS HARDLY A COUNTRY THAT DOES NOT HAVE ITS OWN FAVOURITE LEGUME-BASED DISH, FROM BOSTON BAKED BEANS IN THE USA TO LENTIL DHAL IN INDIA. IN MEXICO, THEY ARE SPICED AND USED TO MAKE REFRIED BEANS, WHILE IN CHINA THEY ARE FERMENTED FOR BLACK BEAN AND YELLOW BEAN SAUCES.

LENTILS AND PEAS

The humble lentil is one of our oldest foods. It originated in Asia and north Africa and continues to be cultivated in those regions, as well as in France and Italy. Lentils are hard even when fresh, so they are always sold dried. Unlike most other pulses, they do not need soaking.

Red Lentils

Orange-coloured red split lentils, sometimes known as Egyptian lentils or masoor dal, are the most familiar variety. They cook in just 20 minutes, eventually disintegrating into a thick purée. They are ideal for thickening soups and casseroles and, when cooked with spices, make a delicious dhal. In the Middle East, red or yellow lentils are cooked and mixed with spices and vegetables to form balls known as *kofte*.

Yellow Lentils

Less well-known yellow lentils taste very similar to the red variety and are used in much the same way.

Green and Brown Lentils

Also referred to as continental lentils, these disc-shaped pulses retain their shape when cooked. They take longer to cook than split lentils – about 40–45 minutes – and are ideal for adding to warm salads, casseroles and stuffings. Alternatively, green and brown lentils can be cooked and blended with herbs or spices to make a nutritious pâté.

Puy Lentils

These tiny, dark, blue-green, marbled lentils grow in the Auvergne region in central France. They are considered to be far superior in taste and texture than other varieties, and they retain their bead-like shape during cooking, which takes around 20–30 minutes. Puy lentils are a delicious addition to simple dishes, such as warm salads, and are good braised in wine and flavoured with herbs.

Umbrian Lentils

These golden-brown Italian lentils are often cooked with onion, garlic and herbs, and served with pasta or rice.

Peas

Dried peas come from the field pea not the garden pea, which is eaten fresh. Unlike lentils, peas are soft when young and require drying. They are available whole or split; the latter have a sweeter flavour and cook more quickly. Like split lentils, split peas do not hold their shape when cooked, making them perfect for dhals, purées, casseroles and soups. They take about 45 minutes to cook.

Right: Green and brown lentils.

Below: Puy lentils.

Left: Red lentils.

COOKING LENTILS

Lentils are easy to cook and don't need to be soaked. Split red and green lentils have a soft consistency when cooked, while whole lentils hold their shape when cooked.

Green, Brown and Puy Lentils

1 Place 250g/9oz/generous 1 cup whole green, brown or puy lentils in a sieve and rinse well under cold running water. Drain, then tip the lentils into a pan.

2 Cover with water and bring to the boil. Simmer for 25–30 minutes until tender, replenishing the water if necessary. Drain and season with salt and freshly ground black pepper.

Split Red and Yellow Lentils

1 Place 250g/9oz/generous 1 cup split lentils in a sieve and rinse thoroughly under cold running water. Drain, then tip the lentils into a pan.

2 Cover with 600ml/1 pint/2½ cups water and bring to the boil. Simmer for 20–25 minutes, stirring occasionally, until the water is absorbed and the lentils are tender. Season to taste.

PEANUTS

Not strictly a nut but a member of the pulse family, peanuts bury themselves just below the earth after flowering – hence their alternative name, groundnuts. They are a staple food in many countries, and are widely used in South-east Asia, notably for satay sauce, and in African cuisines, where they are used as an ingredient in stews. In the West, peanuts are a popular snack food; the shelled nuts are frequently sold roasted and salted, and they are used to make peanut butter. Peanuts are particularly high in fat and are best eaten in moderation.

Buying and Storing Legumes: Lentils and peas toughen with time. Buy from shops with a fast turnover of stock and store in airtight containers in a cool, dark place. Look for bright, unwrinkled pulses. Rinse before use.

Health Benefits of Legumes: Lentils and peas have an impressive range of nutrients including iron, selenium, folate, manganese, zinc, phosphorus and some B vitamins. Extremely low in fat and richer in protein than most pulses, they are reputed to be important in fighting heart disease by reducing harmful low density lipoprotein (LDL) cholesterol in the body. They are high in fibre, which aids the functioning of the bowels and colon, and provide the body with a steady supply of energy.

Above and right: Yellow and green split peas.

Left: Marrow fat peas.

PULSES

THE EDIBLE SEEDS FROM PLANTS BELONGING TO THE LEGUME FAMILY, PULSES, WHICH INCLUDE CHICKPEAS AND A VAST RANGE OF BEANS, ARE PACKED WITH PROTEIN, VITAMINS, MINERALS AND FIBRE, AND ARE EXTREMELY LOW IN FAT. FOR THE COOK, THEIR ABILITY TO ABSORB THE FLAVOURS OF OTHER FOODS MEANS THAT PULSES CAN BE USED AS THE BASE FOR AN INFINITE NUMBER OF DISHES. MOST PULSES REQUIRE SOAKING OVERNIGHT IN COLD WATER BEFORE USE, SO IT IS WISE TO PLAN AHEAD IF USING THE DRIED TYPE; ALTERNATIVELY, CANNED ARE VERY CONVENIENT.

Above: Aduki beans.

Black Beans

These shiny, black, kidney-shaped beans are often used in Caribbean cooking. They have a sweetish flavour, and their distinctive colour adds a dramatic touch to soups, mixed bean salads or casseroles.

Aduki Beans

Also known as adzuki beans, these tiny, deep-red beans have a sweet, nutty flavour and are popular in Oriental dishes. In Chinese cooking, they form the base of a red bean paste. Known as the "king of beans" in Japan, the aduki bean is reputed to be good for the liver and kidneys. They cook quickly and can be used in casseroles and bakes. They are also ground into flour for use in cakes, breads and pastries.

Black-eyed Beans

Known as black-eye peas or cow peas in the USA, black-eyed beans are an essential ingredient in Creole cooking and some spicy Indian curries. The small, creamy-coloured bean is characterized by the black spot on its

Black beans (above) black-eyed beans (above right) and borlotti beans.

CANNELLINI BEAN PURÉE

Cooked cannellini beans make a delicious herb- and garlic-flavoured purée. Serve spread on toasted pitta bread or to use as a dip with chunky raw vegetable crudités.

<u>SERVES FOUR</u>

INGREDIENTS
400g/14oz/2½ cups canned or 200g/7oz/1¼ cups dried
  cannellini beans
30ml/2 tbsp olive oil
2 large garlic cloves, finely chopped
2 shallots, finely chopped
75ml/5 tbsp vegetable stock
30ml/2 tbsp chopped fresh flat
  leaf parsley
15ml/1 tbsp chopped fresh chives
salt and freshly ground black
  pepper

1 If using dried beans, soak them overnight in cold water, then drain and rinse. Place in a pan and cover with cold water, then bring to the boil and boil rapidly for 10 minutes. Reduce the heat and simmer for about 1 hour, or until tender. If using canned beans, rinse and drain well.

2 Heat the oil in a pan and sauté the garlic and shallots for about 5 minutes, stirring occasionally, until soft. Add the beans, stock, parsley and seasoning, then cook for a few minutes until heated through.

3 To make a course purée, mash the beans with a potato masher. Alternatively, place in a food processor and blend until thick and smooth. Serve sprinkled with chopped chives.

Right: Butter beans.

THE F WORD

Many people are put off eating beans due to their unfortunate side effects. The propensity of beans to cause flatulence stems from the gases they produce in the gut. This can be reduced by following these guidelines:

• Never cook pulses in their soaking water as it contains indigestible sugars.

• Skim off any scum that forms on the surface of the water during cooking.

• Add "digestive" spices, such as dill, asafoetida, ginger and caraway, to the cooking water.

THE FLATULENCE-FREE BEAN

The American space programme NASA is involved in research into flatulence-free foods. One such food is the manteca bean. This small, yellow bean is flatulence-free and easy to digest. It is now being grown both in England and the Channel Islands, and should become more widely available.

side where it was once attached to the pod. Good in soups and salads, they can also be added to savoury bakes and casseroles, and can be used in place of haricot (navy) or cannellini beans in a wide variety of dishes.

Borlotti Beans

These oval beans have a red-streaked, pinkish-brown skin and a bitter-sweet flavour. When cooked, they have a tender, moist texture, which is good in Italian bean and pasta soups, as well as hearty vegetable stews. In most recipes, they are interchangeable with red kidney beans.

Broad (Fava) Beans

These large beans were first cultivated by the ancient Egyptians. Usually eaten in

Right: Broad beans.

their fresh form, broad beans change in colour from green to brown when dried, making them difficult to recognize in their dried state. The outer skin can be very tough and chewy, and some people prefer to remove it after cooking. They can also be bought ready-skinned.

Butter Beans and Lima Beans

Similar in flavour and appearance, both butter beans and lima beans are characterized by their flattish, kidney shape and soft, floury texture. Cream-coloured butter beans are familiar in Britain and Greece, while lima beans are popular in the USA.

In Greek cooking, large butter beans, called gigantes, are oven-baked with

tomato, garlic and olive oil until tender and creamy. The pale-green lima bean is used in succotash, an American dish that also includes corn kernels. Butter and lima beans are also good with creamy herb sauces. Care should be taken not to overcook both butter and lima beans as they become pulpy and mushy in texture.

Left: Cannellini beans.

Cannellini Beans

These small, white, kidney-shaped beans have a soft, creamy texture when cooked and are popular in Italian cooking. They can be used in place of haricot (navy) beans and, when dressed with olive oil, lemon juice, crushed garlic and fresh chopped parsley, make an excellent warm salad.

Chickpeas

Also known as garbanzo beans, robust and hearty chickpeas resemble shelled hazelnuts and have a delicious nutty flavour and creamy texture. They need lengthy cooking and are much used in Mediterranean and Middle Eastern cooking – falafel and hummus being two of the most popular dishes made from chickpeas. In India, they are known as gram and are ground into flour to make fritters and flat breads. Gram flour, also called besan, can be found in health food shops and Asian grocery stores.

Flageolet Beans

These young haricot beans are removed from the pod before they are fully ripe, hence their fresh delicate flavour. A pretty, mint-green colour, they are the most expensive bean to buy and are best treated simply. Cook them until they are tender, then season and drizzle with a little olive oil and lemon juice.

Above:
Chickpeas.

Haricot (Navy) Beans

Most commonly used for canned baked beans, these versatile, ivory-coloured beans are small and oval in shape. Called navy or Boston beans in the USA, they suit slow-cooked dishes, such as casseroles and bakes.

Pinto Beans

A smaller, paler version of the borlotti bean, the savoury-tasting pinto has an attractive speckled skin – it is aptly called the painted bean. One of the many relatives of the kidney bean, pinto beans feature extensively in Mexican cooking, most familiarly in refried beans, when they are cooked until tender and fried with garlic, chilli and tomatoes. The beans are then mashed, resulting in a wonderful, spicy, rough purée that is usually served with warm tortillas. Soured cream and garlic-flavoured guacamole are good accompaniments.

Red Kidney Beans

Glossy, mahogany-red kidney beans retain their colour and shape when cooked. They have a soft, "mealy" texture and are much used in South American cooking. An essential ingredient in spicy chillies, they can also be used to make refried beans (although this dish is traditionally made from pinto beans). Cooked kidney beans can be used to make a variety of salads, but they are especially good combined

Above: Clockwise from left: Haricot beans, red kidney beans, flagolet beans and pinto beans.

with red onion and chopped flat leaf parsley and mint, then tossed in an olive oil dressing.

It is essential to follow the cooking instructions when preparing kidney beans as they contain a substance that causes severe food poisoning if they are not boiled vigorously for 10–15 minutes.

COOKING KIDNEY BEANS

Most types of beans, with the exception of aduki beans and mung beans, require soaking for 5–6 hours or overnight and then boiling rapidly for 10–15 minutes to remove any harmful toxins. This is important for kidney beans, which can cause serious food poisoning if not treated in this way.

1 Wash the beans well, then place in a bowl that allows plenty of room for expansion. Cover with cold water and leave to soak overnight or for 8–12 hours, then drain and rinse.

2 Place the beans in a large pan and cover with fresh cold water. Bring to the boil and boil rapidly for 10–15 minutes, then reduce the heat and simmer for 30 minutes to 2 hours, until tender, depending on the type of bean. Drain and serve.

Ful Medames

A member of the broad (fava) bean family, these small Egyptian beans form the base of the national dish of the same name, in which they are flavoured with ground cumin and then baked with olive oil, garlic and lemon, and served topped with hard-boiled egg. They have a strong, nutty flavour and tough, light brown outer skin. Ful medames need to be soaked overnight in cold water, then cooked slowly for about 1½ hours until soft.

Below: Ful medames.

Soya Beans

These small, oval beans vary in colour from creamy-yellow through brown to black. In China, they are known as "meat of the earth" and were once considered sacred. Soya beans contain all the nutritional properties of animal products but without the disadvantages. They are extremely dense and need to be soaked for 12 hours before cooking. They combine well with robust ingredients, such as garlic, herbs and spices, and they make a healthy addition to soups, casseroles, bakes and salads.

Soya beans are also used to make tofu, tempeh, textured vegetable protein (TVP), flour and soy sauce.

Above: White and black soya beans.

HOW TO PREPARE AND COOK PULSES

There is much debate as to whether soaking pulses before cooking is necessary, but it certainly reduces cooking times, and can enhance flavour by starting the germination process. First, wash pulses under cold running water, then place in a bowl of fresh cold water and leave to soak overnight. Discard any pulses that float to the surface, drain and rinse again. Put in a large pan and cover with fresh cold water. Boil rapidly for 10–15 minutes, then reduce the heat, cover and simmer until tender.

COOKING TIMES FOR PULSES

As cooking times can vary depending on the age of the pulses, this table should be used as a general guide.

Aduki beans	30–45 minutes
Black beans	1 hour
Black-eyed beans	1–1¼ hours
Borlotti beans	1–1½ hours
Broad beans	1–1½ hours
Butter/lima beans	1–1¼ hours
Cannellini beans	1 hour
Chickpeas	1½–2½ hours
Flageolet beans	1½ hours
Ful medames	1½ hours
Haricot beans	1–1½ hours
Kidney beans	1–1½ hours
Mung beans	25–40 minutes
Pinto beans	1–1¼ hours
Soya beans	2 hours or more

Mung Beans

Instantly recognizable in their sprouted form as beansprouts, mung or moong beans are small, olive-coloured beans native to India. They are soft and sweet when cooked, and are used in the spicy curry, moong dhal. In several Asian countries mung bean ice cream or ice lollies are popular, as is a "porridge-like" dish in Indonesia. Mung beans are also used to make transparent cellophane noodles, also called glass noodles. Soaking is not essential, but if they are soaked overnight this will reduce the usual 40 minutes cooking time by about half.

Left: Mung beans.

USING CANNED BEANS

Canned beans are convenient store-cupboard stand-bys, because they require no soaking or lengthy cooking. Choose canned beans that do not have added sugar or salt, and rinse well and drain before use. The canning process, according to recent research can help to retain certain nutrients such as calcium and vitamin E.

Canned beans tend to be softer than cooked dried beans so they are easy to mash, which makes them good for pâtés, stuffings, croquettes and rissoles, and they can also be used to make quick salads. They can, in fact, be used for any dish that calls for cooked, dried beans: a drained 425g/15oz can is roughly the equivalent of 150g/5oz/¾ cup dried beans. Firmer canned beans, such as kidney beans can be added to stews and re-cooked, but softer beans, such as flageolet, should be just heated through.

Tepary Beans

Native to Southwest America and Mexico, the name tepary derives from the Papago phrase *t'pawi* or "it's a bean". Cooked teparies are light and mealy, while in their uncooked state they can be toasted then ground into a meal and mixed with water.

Urd Beans

Also known as black gram, the urd is thought to be native to India where it is used to make different purées or dhal. The blackish seeds are similar in size and shape to the mung bean and are also sold whole, split and skinned.

Pigeon Peas

The cultivation of the pigeon pea goes back 3,000 years, probably to Asia. Today, they are widely cultivated in India, Africa and Central America. In India it is one of the most important pulses, next to chickpeas, where they are used to make dhal or they are combined with grains.

Buying and Storing Pulses: Look for plump, shiny beans with an unbroken skin. Beans toughen with age so, although they will keep for up to a year in a cool, dry place, it is best to buy them in small quantities from shops with a regular turnover of stock. Avoid beans that look dusty or dirty and store them in an airtight container.

Health Benefits of Pulses: Beans are packed with protein, soluble and insoluble fibre, iron, potassium, phosphorous, manganese, magnesium, folate and most B vitamins. Soya beans are the most nutritious of all beans. Rich in high-quality protein, this wonder-pulse contains all eight essential amino acids that cannot be synthesized by the body but are vital for the renewal of cells and tissues. Insoluble fibre ensures regular bowel movements, while soluble fibre has been found to lower blood cholesterol, thereby reducing the risk of heart disease and stroke. Studies show that eating pulses on a regular basis can lower cholesterol levels by almost 20 per cent. Beans contain a concentration of lignins, known as phytoestrogens, which protect against cancer of the breast, prostate and colon. Lignins may help to balance hormone levels in the body.

QUICK COOKING AND SERVING IDEAS FOR PULSES

• To flavour beans, add an onion, garlic, herbs or spices before cooking. Remove whole items before serving.

• Spoon spicy, red lentil dhal and some crisp, fried onions on top of a warm tortilla, then roll up and eat.

• Dress cooked beans with extra virgin olive oil, lemon juice, crushed garlic, diced tomato and fresh basil.

• Mix cooked chickpeas with spring onions (scallions), olives and chopped parsley, then drizzle over olive oil and add lemon juice.

• Mash cooked beans with olive oil, garlic and coriander. Pile on to toasted bread. Top with a poached egg.

• Fry cooked red kidney beans in olive oil with chopped onion, chilli, garlic and fresh coriander (cilantro) leaves.

• Sauté some chopped garlic in olive oil, add canned flageolet beans, canned tomatoes and chopped fresh chilli, then cook for a few minutes until the sauce has thickened slightly and the beans are heated through.

• Roast cooked chickpeas, which have been drizzled with olive oil and garlic, for 20 minutes at 200°C/400°F/Gas 6, then toss in a little ground cumin and sprinkle with chilli flakes. Serve with chunks of feta cheese and naan bread.

SPROUTED BEANS AND LENTILS

SPROUTS ARE QUITE REMARKABLE IN TERMS OF THEIR NUTRITIONAL CONTENT. ONCE THE BEAN OR GRAIN HAS GERMINATED OR SPROUTED, THE NUTRITIONAL VALUE RISES DRAMATICALLY. THERE ARE ALMOST 30 PER CENT MORE B VITAMINS AND 60 PER CENT MORE VITAMIN C IN THE SPROUT THAN IN THE ORIGINAL BEAN, LENTIL OR GRAIN. SUPERMARKETS AND HEALTH FOOD SHOPS SELL A VARIETY OF SPROUTS, BUT IT IS EASY TO GROW THEM AT HOME — ALL YOU NEED IS A JAR, A PIECE OF MUSLIN AND AN ELASTIC BAND.

Beansprouts or Mung Beansprouts

The most commonly available beansprouts, these have long, translucent white shoots and are popular in Chinese and Asian cooking, where they are used in soups, salads and stir-fries. They have a crunchy texture and a delicate flavour. Bought varieties tend to be larger than home sprouted.

Below: Mung beansprouts.

Wheat Berry Sprouts

Sprouts grown from wheat berries have a crunchy texture and sweet flavour and are excellent in breads. If they are left to grow, the sprouts will become wheat-grass, a powerful detoxifier that it is often made into a juice.

Chickpea Sprouts

Sprouts grown from chickpeas have a nutty flavour and are substantial in size. Use in salads and stews.

Lentil Sprouts

These sprouts have a slightly spicy, peppery flavour and thin, white shoots. Use only whole lentils: split ones won't sprout.

Aduki Bean Sprouts

These fine wispy sprouts have a sweet nutty taste. Use in salads, stir-fries, bakes and stews.

Buying and Storing Sprouts: If you can, choose fresh, crisp sprouts with the bean, lentil or grain still attached. Avoid any that are slimy or musty-looking. Sprouts are best eaten on the day they are bought but, if fresh, they will keep, wrapped in a plastic container or clean, dry jar, in the refrigerator for 2–6 days. Rinse and pat dry before use.

Health Benefits of Sprouts: Sprouted beans, lentils and grains supply rich amounts of protein, B vitamins and vitamins C and E, calcium, iron, potassium and phosphorus, which, due to the sprouting process, are in an easily digestible form. Sprouting also boosts the enzyme content. Plant enzymes are said to boost the metabolism and are good for the skin, stress and fatigue. In Chinese medicine, sprouts are highly valued for their ability to cleanse and rejuvenate the system.

SPROUTING BEANS AND LENTILS

Larger pulses, such as chickpeas and whole grains, take longer to sprout than small beans, but they are all simple to grow and are usually ready to eat in 2–4 days. Store sprouts in a covered container in the refrigerator for 2–6 days.

2 The next day, pour off the water through the muslin and fill the jar again with water. Shake gently, then turn the jar upside down and drain thoroughly. Leave the jar on its side in a warm place, away from direct sunlight. The ideal temperature is 17–24°C.

1 Wash 45ml/3 tbsp beans, lentils or grains thoroughly in water, then place in a large jar. Fill the jar with lukewarm water, cover with a piece of muslin (cheesecloth) and fasten securely with an elastic band. Leave in a draught-free place to stand overnight.

3 Rinse the beans, lentils or grains gently but thoroughly three times a day, for 2–4 days. Make sure they are drained thoroughly to prevent them from turning mouldy. Remove the sprouts from the jar, rinse well and remove any ungerminated beans.

HOW TO USE SPROUTS

- Try combining different types of sprouted beans and grains for a range of textures and flavours. They add a crunchy texture to salads and sandwich fillings.
- Mung beansprouts are often used in Oriental food, particularly stir-fries, and require little cooking.
- Alfalfa sprouts, which derive from a seed, are another popular sprout. They have tiny, wispy white sprouts and a mild nutty flavour.
- Sprouted grains are good in breads, adding a pleasant crunchy texture. Knead them in after the first rising, before shaping the loaf.
- Use chickpea and lentil sprouts in casseroles and bakes.

Right: Wheat berry sprouts.

Right: Chickpea sprouts.

Right: Lentil sprouts.

Right: Aduki bean sprouts.

TIPS ON SPROUTING

- If you are growing your own sprouts, it's important to buy beans, lentils or grains that are specifically for sprouting, rather than cooking.
- Use whole beans, lentils and grains as split or processed ones will not germinate.
- Regular rinsing with fresh water and thorough draining is essential when sprouting to prevent the beans from turning rancid and mouldy.
- Cover the sprouting jar with muslin to allow air to circulate and to let water in and out.
- After two or three days, the jar can be placed near sunlight (but not hot sun) to encourage the green pigment chlorophyll and increase the sprout's magnesium and fibre content.
- Soya beans and chickpea sprouts need to be rinsed four times a day.
- Keen sprouters may wish to invest in a special sprouting container that comes with a number of holes in the base for easy draining.
- The soaking water is said to be very nutritious and can be drunk, if liked.

Below: Germinating sprouts.

SOYA BEAN PRODUCTS

SOYA BEANS ARE INCREDIBLY VERSATILE AND ARE USED TO MAKE AN EXTENSIVE ARRAY OF BY-PRODUCTS, INCLUDING TOFU, TEMPEH, TEXTURED VEGETABLE PROTEIN (TVP), FLOUR, MISO, AND A VARIETY OF SAUCES. THE SOYA BEAN IS THE MOST NUTRITIOUS OF ALL BEANS. RICH IN HIGH-QUALITY PROTEIN, IT IS ONE OF THE FEW VEGETARIAN FOODS THAT CONTAINS ALL EIGHT ESSENTIAL AMINO ACIDS THAT CANNOT BE SYNTHESIZED IN THE BODY AND ARE VITAL FOR THE RENEWAL OF CELLS AND TISSUES.

TOFU

Also known as beancurd, tofu is made in a similar way to soft cheese. The beans are boiled, mashed and sieved to make soya "milk", and the "milk" is then curdled using a coagulant. The resulting curds are drained and pressed to make tofu, and there are several different types to choose from.

Firm Tofu

This type of tofu is sold in blocks and can be cubed or sliced and used in vegetable stir-fries, kebabs, salads, soups and casseroles. Alternatively, firm tofu can be mashed and used in bakes and burgers. The mild flavour of firm tofu is improved by marinating, since its porous texture readily absorbs flavours and seasonings.

Silken Tofu

Soft blocks with a silky, smooth texture, this type of tofu is ideal for use in sauces, dressings, dips and soups. It is a useful dairy-free alternative to cream, soft cheese or yogurt, and can be used to make creamy desserts.

OTHER FORMS OF TOFU

Smoked, marinated and deep-fried tofu are all readily available in health food stores and some supermarkets.

Deep-fried tofu is often used in Chinese dishes. It puffs up during cooking and, underneath the golden, crisp coating the tofu is white and soft, and easily absorbs the flavour of other ingredients. It can be used in much the same way as firm tofu and, as it has been fried in vegetable oil, it is suitable for vegetarian cooking.

Buying and Storing Tofu: All types of fresh tofu can be kept in the refrigerator for up to one week. Firm tofu should be kept covered in water, which must be changed regularly. Freezing tofu is not recommended, because it alters its texture. Silken tofu is often available in long-life vacuum packs, which do not have to be kept in the refrigerator and have a much longer shelf life.

TEMPEH

This Indonesian speciality is made by fermenting cooked soya beans with a cultured starter. Tempeh is similar to tofu but has a nuttier, more savoury flavour and a firmer texture. It can be used in the same way as firm tofu and also benefits from marinating. While some types of tofu are regarded as a dairy replacement, the firmer texture of tempeh means that it can be used instead of meat in pies and casseroles.

Buying and Storing Tempeh: Tempeh is available chilled or frozen in health food stores and oriental shops, and can be ready marinated. Chilled tempeh can be stored in the refrigerator for up to a week. Frozen tempeh can be left in the freezer for one month; defrost before use.

BEANCURD SKINS AND STICKS

Made from soya "milk", dried beancurd skins and sticks, like fresh beancurd, have neither aroma nor flavour until they are cooked, when they will rapidly absorb the flavour of seasonings and

Above: Clockwise from left: silken tofu, beancurd skins, firm tofu and deep fried tofu.

Left: Tempeh.

TVP

Textured vegetable protein, or TVP, is a useful meat replacement and is usually bought in dry chunks or as mince. Made from processed soya beans, TVP is very versatile and readily absorbs the strong flavours of ingredients, such as herbs, spices and vegetable stock. It is inexpensive and is a convenient store-cupboard item. TVP needs to be rehydrated in boiling water or vegetable stock, and can be used in stews and curries, or as a filling for pies.

other ingredients. Beancurd skins and sticks are used in Chinese cooking and need to be soaked until pliable before use. Beancurd skins should be soaked in cold water for an hour or two and can be used to wrap a variety of fillings.

Beancurd sticks need to be soaked for several hours or overnight. They can be chopped and added to soups, stir-fries and casseroles.

MARINATED TOFU KEBABS

Tofu is relatively tasteless but its great advantage is that it readily takes on other flavours. It is at its best when marinated in aromatic oils, soy sauce, Asian pastes or sauces, spices and herbs.

1 Cut a block of tofu into 1cm/½in cubes and marinate in a mixture of groundnut (peanut) oil, sesame oil, soy sauce, crushed garlic, grated fresh root ginger and honey for at least 1 hour.

2 Thread the cubes of tofu on to skewers with chunks of courgettes (zucchini), onions and mushrooms. Brush with the marinade and grill (broil) or barbecue until golden, turning occasionally.

TOFU FRUIT FOOL

1 Place a packet of silken tofu in the bowl of a food processor. Add some soft fruit, such as berries – for example, strawberries, raspberries or blackberries.

2 Process the mixture to form a smooth purée, then sweeten to taste with a little honey, maple syrup or maize malt syrup.

Left: Soya flour.

SOYA FLOUR

This is a finely ground, high-protein flour, which is also gluten-free. It is often mixed with other flours in bread and pastries, adding a pleasant nuttiness, or it can be used as a thickener in sauces.

Buying and Storing TVP and Soya Flour: Store TVP and soya flour in an airtight container in a cool, dry, dark place.

Soy Sauce

This soya by-product originated more than 2,000 years ago and the recipe has changed little since then. It is made by combining crushed soya beans with wheat, salt, water and a yeast-based culture called koji. The mixture is left to ferment for between 6 months and 3 years.

There are two basic types of soy sauce: light and dark. Light soy sauce is slightly thinner in consistency but it is saltier. It is used in dressings, soups and stir-fries. Dark soy sauce is heavier and sweeter, with a more rounded flavour, and is used in marinades, stir-fries and sauces. Buy naturally brewed soy sauce as many other kinds are now chemically prepared to hasten the fermentation process, and may contain flavourings and colourings.

Shoyu

Made in Japan, shoyu is aged for 1–2 years to produce a full-flavoured sauce that can be used in the same way as dark soy sauce. Buy it in health food stores and oriental shops.

Tamari

This form of soy sauce is a natural by-product of making miso, although it is often produced in the same way as soy sauce. Most tamari is made without wheat, which means that it is gluten-free. It has a rich, dark, robust flavour and is used in cooking or as a condiment.

Buying and Storing Soy Sauce, Shoyu and Tamari: Keep soy sauce, shoyu and tamari in a cool, dark place.

MISO

This thick paste is made from a mixture of cooked soya beans, rice, wheat or barley, salt and water. Miso is then left to ferment for up to 3 years. It can be used to add a savoury flavour to soups, stocks, stir-fries and noodle dishes, and is a staple food in Asia. There are three main types: kome, or white miso, is the lightest and sweetest; medium-strength

SOYA BEAN SAUCES

Black bean sauce: Made from fermented black soya beans, this has a rich, thick consistency and a salty, full flavour. It should always be heated before use to bring out the flavour. Fermented black beans, which Chinese cooks use to make home-made black bean sauce, can be bought in vacuum-packs or cans from oriental shops. They need rinsing before use.

Yellow bean sauce: Produced from fermented yellow soya beans, this sauce has an intense flavour.

Hoisin sauce: A thick red-brown sauce made from soya beans, flour, garlic, chilli, sesame oil and vinegar. Mainly intended as a marinade, it can also be used as a dipping sauce.

Kecap manis: An Indonesian-style dark, sweet soy sauce, which can be found in oriental shops.

Above: Minced and cubed textured vegetable protein (TVP).

mugi miso, which has a mellow flavour and is preferred for everyday use; and hacho miso, which is dark chocolate in colour, has a thick texture and a strong flavour.

Buying and Storing Miso: Miso keeps well and can be stored for several months, but should be kept in the refrigerator once it has been opened.

Health Benefits of Soya Products: Soya is often hailed for its health benefits. Rich in minerals, particularly iron and calcium, it is also low in saturated fat and is cholesterol-free. Some soya products are thought to help reduce osteoporosis, blood pressure and blood cholesterol, and there is evidence to suggest that it can help reduce the risk of cancer.

Japanese women (whose diets include soya) have a lower incidence of breast cancer than women who consume a typical Western diet. Likewise, Japanese men have a lower incidence of prostate cancer than Western men. This is thought to be because soya contains hormone-like substances called phytoestrogens.

Studies have also shown that eating miso on a regular basis can increase the body's natural resistance to radiation. Additionally, miso is said to help prevent cancer of the liver, and it can also help to expel toxins from the body.

Below: Light soy sauce and dark soy sauce (right) .

WATCH POINT
Although soya beans and products are nutritionally beneficial, they are also common allergens and can provoke reactions such as headaches and digestive problems. Avoid eating excessive amounts of soya, and always cook sprouted soya beans before use.

Left: Mugi miso (left) and hacho miso.

Above: Tamari (left) and shoyu.

APPETIZERS
AND SOUPS

*The selection of recipes in this chapter traverse
the globe, from a filling Spanish-style Bean
Omelette for any time of day, to Middle Eastern
Falafel, Italian Bean Ribollita and distinctive
Spicy Peanut Soup. Many of these dishes would
make a substantial meal for one, and all contain
nutritious and healthy ingredients.*

CANNELLINI BEAN BRUSCHETTA

THIS DISH IS A SOPHISTICATED VERSION OF BEANS ON TOAST. CANNELLINI BEANS HAVE A DELICATE FLAVOUR AND SOFT TEXTURE THAT MELDS WELL WITH MORE INTENSE INGREDIENTS SUCH AS SUN-DRIED TOMATOES, GARLIC AND BASIL.

SERVES FOUR

INGREDIENTS

150g/5oz/²/₃ cup dried cannellini
  beans
5 fresh tomatoes
45ml/3 tbsp olive oil, plus extra
  for drizzling
2 sun-dried tomatoes in oil, drained
  and finely chopped
2 garlic cloves
30ml/2 tbsp chopped fresh rosemary
salt and ground black pepper
a handful of fresh basil leaves,
  to garnish
12 slices Italian-style bread, such
  as ciabatta

1 Place the beans in a large bowl and cover with water. Leave to soak overnight. Drain and rinse the beans, then place in a pan and cover with fresh water. Bring to the boil and boil rapidly for 10 minutes. Reduce the heat and simmer for 50–60 minutes or until tender. Drain and set aside.

2 Meanwhile, place the tomatoes in a bowl, cover with boiling water, leave for 30 seconds, then peel, seed and chop the flesh. Heat the oil in a frying pan, add the fresh and sun-dried tomatoes. Crush 1 garlic clove into the pan and add the rosemary. Cook for 2 minutes until the tomatoes begin to break down and soften.

3 Add the tomato mixture to the cannellini beans, season to taste and mix well. Reheat gently.

COOK'S TIP
Canned beans can be used instead of dried; use 275g/10oz/2 cups drained and rinsed canned beans and add to the tomato mixture in step 3.

4 Cut the remaining garlic clove in half. Rub the cut sides of the bread slices with the garlic clove, then toast lightly. Spoon the cannellini bean mixture on top of the toast. Sprinkle with basil leaves and drizzle with a little extra olive oil before serving.

Energy 479kcal/2026kJ; Protein 19.9g; Carbohydrate 74.8g, of which sugars 10.3g; Fat 13.3g, of which saturates 2g; Cholesterol 0mg; Calcium 173mg; Fibre 10.2g; Sodium 563mg.

SPANISH-STYLE BEAN OMELETTE

ALMOST REGARDED AS THE NATIONAL DISH OF SPAIN, THE TRADITIONAL SPANISH OMELETTE CONSISTS SIMPLY OF POTATOES, ONIONS AND EGGS. THIS ONE HAS CANNELLINI BEANS, TOO, AND MAKES A VERY SUBSTANTIAL VEGETARIAN SNACK.

SERVES SIX

INGREDIENTS
30ml/2 tbsp olive oil, plus extra
  for drizzling
1 Spanish onion, chopped
1 small red (bell) pepper, seeded
  and diced
2 celery sticks, chopped
225g/8oz potatoes, peeled, diced
  and cooked
400g/14oz can cannellini
  beans, drained and rinsed
8 eggs
salt and ground black pepper
sprigs of oregano, to garnish
green salad and olives, to serve

4 Stir the egg mixture with a wooden spatula until it begins to thicken, then allow it to cook over a low heat for about 8 minutes. The omelette should be firm, but still moist in the middle.

5 Cool slightly then invert on to a serving plate. Cut the omelette into thick wedges. Serve warm or cool with a green salad and olives and a little olive oil. Garnish with oregano.

1 Heat the olive oil in a frying pan. Add the onion, red pepper and celery, and cook for 3–5 minutes until the vegetables are soft, but not coloured.

2 Add the potatoes and beans, and cook for several minutes.

3 In a small bowl, beat the eggs with a fork, then season well and pour over the ingredients in the pan.

Energy 252kcal/1055kJ; Protein 14.5g; Carbohydrate 23.8g, of which sugars 7.6g; Fat 11.8g, of which saturates 2.7g; Cholesterol 254mg; Calcium 107mg; Fibre 5.8g; Sodium 366mg.

BROAD BEAN DIP WITH PAPRIKA

THIS GARLICKY BROAD BEAN DIP IS ENJOYED THROUGHOUT MOROCCO. SPRINKLED WITH PAPRIKA OR DRIED THYME, IT MAKES A TASTY APPETIZER SERVED WITH FLAT BREAD.

SERVES FOUR

INGREDIENTS
   350g/12oz/1¾ cups dried broad
    (fava) beans, soaked overnight
   4 garlic cloves
   10ml/2 tsp cumin seeds
   60–75ml/4–5 tbsp olive oil
   salt
   paprika or dried thyme, to garnish

COOK'S TIP
Broad (fava) beans are a popular
ingredient in North African cooking. They
change colour from green to brown when
dried and have a tough outer skin which
is best removed after soaking or cooking.

1 Drain the beans, remove their wrinkly skins and place them in a large pan with the garlic and cumin seeds. Add enough water to cover the beans and bring to the boil. Boil for 10 minutes, then reduce the heat, cover the pan and simmer gently for about 1 hour, or until the beans are tender.

2 When cooked, drain the beans and, while they are still warm, pound or process them with the olive oil until the mixture forms a smooth dip. Season to taste with salt and serve warm or at room temperature, sprinkled with paprika or thyme. Alternatively, simply drizzle with a little olive oil.

Energy 344kcal/1449kJ; Protein 20.3g; Carbohydrate 40.6g, of which sugars 2.4g; Fat 12.3g, of which saturates 1.8g; Cholesterol 0mg; Calcium 90mg; Fibre 14.3g; Sodium 16mg.

HUMMUS

*BLENDING CHICKPEAS WITH GARLIC AND OIL MAKES A SURPRISINGLY CREAMY PURÉE THAT IS
DELICIOUS AS A DIP WITH VEGETABLES OR SPREAD OVER PITTA BREAD.*

SERVES FOUR TO SIX

INGREDIENTS
  150g/5oz/³⁄₄ cup dried chickpeas
  juice of 2 lemons
  2 garlic cloves, sliced
  30ml/2 tbsp olive oil
  pinch of cayenne pepper
  150ml/¹⁄₄ pint/²⁄₃ cup tahini paste
  salt and ground black pepper
  extra olive oil and cayenne pepper,
   for sprinkling
  flat leaf parsley, to garnish

1 Put the chickpeas in a bowl with plenty of cold water and leave to soak overnight.

2 Drain the chickpeas and cover with fresh water in a pan. Bring to the boil and boil rapidly for 10 minutes. Reduce the heat and simmer gently for about 1 hour until soft. Drain.

3 Put the chickpeas in a blender or food processor and process to a coarse purée. Add the lemon juice, garlic, olive oil, cayenne pepper and tahini and blend until smooth and creamy, scraping the mixture down from the sides of the bowl.

4 Season the purée with salt and pepper and transfer to a serving dish. Sprinkle with oil and cayenne pepper and serve garnished with a few parsley sprigs.

COOK'S TIPS
• For convenience, canned chickpeas can be used instead. Allow two 400g/14oz cans and drain and rinse them thoroughly.
• Tahini paste can now be purchased from most supermarkets or health food shops.
• Add a handful of chopped black olives to the purée.

Energy 202Kcal/845kJ; Protein 11.9g; Carbohydrate 13.1g, of which sugars 2g; Fat 11.8g, of which saturates 4.8g; Cholesterol 87mg; Calcium 59mg; Fibre 1.5g; Sodium 654mg.

CANNELLINI BEAN DIP

SPREAD THIS SOFT BEAN DIP OR PÂTÉ ON WHEATEN CRACKERS OR TOASTED MUFFINS. ALTERNATIVELY, IT CAN BE SERVED WITH WEDGES OF TOMATO AND A FRESH GREEN SALAD.

2 Use a potato masher to roughly purée the beans, then stir in the lemon rind and juice and olive oil.

3 Stir in the garlic and parsley. Add Tabasco sauce and salt and pepper.

4 Spoon the dip into a bowl and dust lightly with cayenne pepper. Chill until ready to serve.

VARIATION
Other beans can be used for this dish, if preferred, for example, butter beans or kidney beans.

SERVES FOUR

INGREDIENTS
  400g/14oz can cannellini beans
  grated rind and juice of 1 lemon
  30ml/2 tbsp olive oil
  1 garlic clove, finely chopped
  30ml/2 tbsp chopped fresh parsley
  red Tabasco sauce, to taste
  cayenne pepper
  salt and ground black pepper

1 Drain the cannellini beans in a sieve and rinse them well under cold running water. Transfer to a shallow bowl.

Energy 155kcal/650kJ; Protein 7.4g; Carbohydrate 18.4g, of which sugars 3.9g; Fat 6.3g, of which saturates 0.9g; Cholesterol 0mg; Calcium 96mg; Fibre 6.9g; Sodium 394mg.

MUSHROOM AND BEAN PÂTÉ

THIS LIGHT AND TASTY PÂTÉ IS DELICIOUS SERVED ON WHOLEMEAL TOAST OR WITH CRUSTY FRENCH BREAD AND MAKES AN EXCELLENT VEGETARIAN APPETIZER OR LIGHT LUNCH SERVED WITH SALAD.

SERVES EIGHT

INGREDIENTS

30ml/2 tbsp vegetable stock
1 onion, finely chopped
2 garlic cloves, crushed
1 red (bell) pepper, seeded and diced
450g/1lb/6 cups mushrooms, sliced
30ml/2 tbsp dry white wine
400g/14oz can red kidney beans,
  drained and rinsed
1 egg, beaten
50g/2oz/1 cup fresh wholemeal
  (whole-wheat) breadcrumbs
10ml/2 tsp chopped fresh thyme
10ml/2 tsp chopped fresh rosemary
salt and ground black pepper
salad leaves, fresh herbs and tomato
  wedges, to garnish

1 Heat the stock in a pan. Add the onion, garlic and pepper, and cook for 15 minutes, stirring occasionally, until softened but not browned.

2 Add the mushrooms. Stir well, cover and cook gently for 15 minutes, until the mushrooms are reduced slightly. Add the wine, stir and then simmer, uncovered, for a further 15 minutes, until the excess liquor has evaporated.

3 Tip the mushroom mixture into a food processor or blender and add the rinsed kidney beans. process to make a smooth purée, stopping the machine once or twice to scrape down the sides.

4 Add the egg to the processor and blend briefly. Finally, add the breadcrumbs, thyme, rosemary and seasoning. Pulse briefly to mix, taking care not to overprocess the mixture.

5 Preheat the oven to 180°C/350°F/ gas 4. Line a 450g/1lb loaf tin (pan) with greaseproof (waxed) paper and grease well.

6 Turn the mixture into the prepared tin and press down well. Cover with greaseproof paper and foil, folding it around the edges of the tin

7 Bake for about 1¼ hours, until the pâté is just firm. Leave to cool completely and then chill for several hours or overnight.

8 To serve, turn the pâté out of the tin, peel off the lining paper and cut into slices. Serve with Melba toast and salad leaves.

VARIATION
To make a lighter, milder-tasting pâté, use cannellini or flageolet beans in place of the kidney beans.

Energy 104kcal/440kJ; Protein 6.6g; Carbohydrate 16.4g, of which sugars 4g; Fat 1.6g, of which saturates 0.3g; Cholesterol 24mg; Calcium 67mg; Fibre 4.7g; Sodium 257mg.

FALAFEL

These spicy fritters can be made using dried broad beans too. They are lovely served with garlicky yogurt or stuffed into warmed pitta bread, with salad, hummus and chilli sauce.

SERVES FOUR

INGREDIENTS

150g/5oz/³⁄₄ cup dried chickpeas
1 large onion, roughly chopped
2 garlic cloves, roughly chopped
60ml/4 tbsp roughly chopped parsley
5ml/1 tsp cumin seeds, crushed
5ml/1 tsp coriander seeds, crushed
2.5ml/½ tsp baking powder
vegetable oil, for deep-frying
salt and ground black pepper
pitta bread, salad and yogurt,
  to serve

1 Put the chickpeas in a bowl with plenty of cold water. Leave to soak overnight.

2 Drain the chickpeas and cover with water in a pan. Bring to the boil. Boil rapidly for 10 minutes. Reduce the heat and simmer for about 1 hour until soft. Drain.

3 Place the chickpeas in a food processor with the onion, garlic, parsley, cumin, coriander and baking powder. Add salt and pepper to taste. Process until the mixture forms a firm paste.

4 Shape the mixture into walnut-size balls and flatten them slightly. In a deep pan, heat 5cm/2in oil until a little of the mixture sizzles on the surface. Fry the falafel in batches until golden. Drain on kitchen paper and keep hot while frying the remainder. Serve warm in pitta bread, with salad and yogurt.

Energy 249kcal/1041kJ; Protein 9.2g; Carbohydrate 24.8g, of which sugars 5.4g; Fat 13.3g, of which saturates 1.5g; Cholesterol 0mg; Calcium 99mg; Fibre 5.6g; Sodium 20mg.

BLACK-EYED BEAN FRITTERS

THESE BLACK-EYED BEAN FRITTERS ARE MADE IN MUCH THE SAME WAY AS FALAFEL. THE MIXTURE CAN BE MADE THE DAY BEFORE COOKING AND REFRIGERATED.

SERVES FOUR

INGREDIENTS
225g/8oz/1¼ cups dried
  black-eyed beans (peas)
1 onion, chopped
1 fresh red chilli, halved, with seeds
  removed (optional)
about 150ml/¼ pint/⅔ cup water
salt and ground black pepper
vegetable oil, for deep-frying

1 Soak the black-eyed beans in plenty of cold water for 6–8 hours or overnight. Drain the beans and then briskly rub them between the palms of your hands to remove the skins.

2 Return the beans to a bowl, top up with water and the skins will float to the surface. Discard the skins and soak the beans again for 2 hours.

3 Place the beans in a blender or food processor with the onion, chilli (if using), and a little water. Process to make a thick paste. Season with salt and pepper. Pour the mixture into a large bowl and whisk for a few minutes.

4 Heat the oil in a large, heavy pan and fry spoonfuls of the mixture for 4 minutes, until golden brown. Serve.

Energy 254kcal/1066kJ; Protein 12.6g; Carbohydrate 26g, of which sugars 2.3g; Fat 11.8g, of which saturates 1.4g; Cholesterol 0mg; Calcium 60mg; Fibre 9.1g; Sodium 11mg.

BLACK BEAN SALSA

THIS SALSA HAS A VERY STRIKING APPEARANCE, COMBINING DISTINCTIVE BLACK BEANS WITH RED CHILLIES, RED ONION AND FRESH CORIANDER. LIKE OTHER MEMBERS OF THE KIDNEY BEAN FAMILY, THEY HAVE A SUCCULENT TEXTURE AND SLIGHT SWEETNESS.

SERVES FOUR

INGREDIENTS

130g/4½oz/generous ½ cup black
  beans, soaked overnight in water
  to cover
1 pasado chilli
2 fresh red Fresno chillies
1 red onion
grated rind and juice of 1 lime
30ml/2 tbsp Mexican beer (optional)
15ml/1 tbsp olive oil
small bunch of fresh coriander,
  (cilantro) chopped
salt

1 Drain the beans and put them in a large pan. Pour in water to cover and bring to the boil and boil for 10 minutes. Reduce the heat, cover and simmer for about 40 minutes or until tender. They should still have a little bite and should not have begun to disintegrate. Drain, rinse under cold water, then drain again and leave the beans until cold.

2 Soak the pasado chilli in hot water for about 10 minutes until softened. Drain, remove the stalk, then slit the chilli and scrape out the seeds with a small sharp knife. Chop the flesh finely.

3 Spear the Fresno chillies on a long-handled metal skewer and roast them over the flame of a gas burner until the skins blister and darken. Do not let the flesh burn. Alternatively, dry-fry them in a griddle pan until the skins are scorched. Then place the roasted chillies in a strong plastic bag and tie the top to keep the steam in. Set aside for 20 minutes.

4 Meanwhile, chop the red onion finely. Remove the chillies from the bag and peel off the skins. Slit them, remove the seeds and chop them finely.

5 Tip the beans into a bowl and add the onion and both types of chilli. Stir in the lime rind and juice, beer, oil and coriander. Season with salt and mix well. Chill for a few hours before serving to allow the flavours to merge.

Energy 121kcal/510kJ; Protein 7.7g; Carbohydrate 15.9g, of which sugars 2g; Fat 3.4g, of which saturates 0.5g; Cholesterol 0mg; Calcium 61mg; Fibre 6g; Sodium 11mg.

PINTO BEAN SALSA

THESE BEANS HAVE A PRETTY, SPECKLED APPEARANCE AND ARE MOST COMMONLY USED TO MAKE THE TRADITIONAL MEXICAN DISH OF REFRIED BEANS. THE SMOKY FLAVOUR OF THE CHIPOTLE CHILLIES AND THE HERBY TASTE OF THE PASILLA CHILLI CONTRAST WELL WITH THE TART TOMATILLOS.

SERVES FOUR

INGREDIENTS
  130g/4½oz/generous ½ cup pinto
    beans, soaked overnight in water
    to cover
  2 chipotle chillies
  1 pasilla chilli
  2 garlic cloves, peeled
  ½ onion
  200g/7oz fresh tomatillos
  salt

1 Drain the beans and put them in a large pan. Pour in water to cover and place the lid on the pan. Bring to the boil, lower the heat slightly and simmer the beans for 45–50 minutes or until tender. They should still have a little bite and should not have begun to disintegrate. Drain, rinse under cold water, then drain again and tip into a bowl. Leave the beans until cold.

2 Soak the chipotle and pasilla chillies in hot water for about 10 minutes until softened. Drain, reserving the soaking water. Remove the stalks, then slit each chilli and scrape out the seeds with a small sharp knife. Chop the flesh finely and mix it to a smooth paste with a little of the soaking water.

COOK'S TIP
Canned tomatillos can be used instead, but to keep a clean, fresh flavour add a little lime juice.

3 Roast the garlic in a dry frying pan over a medium heat for a few minutes until the cloves start to turn golden. Crush them and add them to the beans.

4 Chop the onion and tomatillos and stir them into the beans. Add the chilli paste and mix well. Add salt to taste, cover and chill before serving.

Energy 104kcal/444kJ; Protein 7.9g; Carbohydrate 17.7g, of which sugars 3.8g; Fat 0.7g, of which saturates 0.2g; Cholesterol 0mg; Calcium 42mg; Fibre 6.2g; Sodium 12mg.

DEEP FRIED TOFU

TOFU SHEETS NEED TO BE SOAKED BRIEFLY IN WATER BEFORE FILLING AND FRYING UNTIL CRISP AND GOLDEN. THEY ARE AVAILABLE IN ASIAN SUPERMARKETS.

SERVES FOUR

INGREDIENTS

30ml/2 tbsp groundnut (peanut oil)
50g/2oz fresh enokitake mushrooms, finely chopped
1 garlic clove, crushed
5ml/1 tsp grated fresh root ginger
4 spring onions (scallions), finely shredded
1 small carrot, cut into matchsticks
115g/4oz bamboo shoots, cut into matchsticks
15ml/1 tbsp light soy sauce
5ml/1 tsp chilli sauce
5ml/1 tsp sugar
15ml/1 tbsp cornflour (cornstarch)
8 tofu sheets, 18 x 22cm (7 x 9in)
sunflower oil, for frying

1 Heat the groundnut oil in a wok over a high heat and add the chopped mushrooms, garlic, ginger, spring onions, carrot and bamboo shoots. Stir-fry for 2–3 minutes and add the soy sauce, chilli sauce and sugar and toss to mix thoroughly.

2 Remove the vegetables from the heat and place in a seive to drain the juices. Set aside to cool.

3 In a small bowl, mix the cornflour with 60ml/4 tbsp of cold water to form a smooth paste. Soak the tofu sheets in a bowl of warm water for 10–15 seconds and then lay them out on a clean work surface and pat dry with kitchen paper.

4 Brush the edges of one of the tofu sheets with the cornflour paste and place 30–45ml/2–3 tbsp of the vegetable mixture at one end of the sheet. Fold the edges over towards the centre and roll up tightly to form a neat roll. Repeat with the remaining bean curd sheets and filling.

5 Place the filled rolls on a baking parchment-lined baking sheet or tray, cover and chill for 3–4 hours.

6 To cook, fill a wok one-third full with sunflower oil and heat to 180°C/350°F or until a cube of bread dropped into the oil browns in 15 seconds.

7 Working in batches, deep-fry the rolls for 2–3 minutes, or until crisp and golden. Drain on kitchen paper and serve immediately with crisp salad leaves.

Energy 270kcal/1119kJ; Protein 10.9g; Carbohydrate 7.7g, of which sugars 3.4g; Fat 21.9g, of which saturates 2.6g; Cholesterol 0mg; Calcium 649mg; Fibre 0.8g; Sodium 280mg.

MUNG BEAN SOUFFLÉ PANCAKES

THESE MUNG BEAN PANCAKES ARE DELICIOUSLY LIGHT, FILLED WITH A MOUTHWATERING COMBINATION OF MEAT AND VEGETABLES. THE GARLIC FLAVOURS ARE COMPLEMENTED BY THE SAUCE.

SERVES THREE TO FOUR

INGREDIENTS
  375g/13oz/2 cups mung beans,
    soaked overnight in cold water
  15ml/1 tbsp pine nuts
  30ml/2 tbsp sweet rice flour
  75g/3oz beef flank, sliced
  200g/7oz prawns (shrimp), peeled
    and finely chopped
  15ml/1 tbsp vegetable oil, plus extra
    for shallow frying
  1 button (white) mushroom, thinly
    sliced
  ½ onion, thinly sliced
  ½ cucumber, seeded and sliced
  ½ cup cabbage *kimichi*, thinly sliced
  3 spring onions (scallions), sliced
  1 red chilli, shredded
  salt and ground black pepper
For the marinade
  5ml/1 tsp mirin or rice wine
  2.5ml/½ tsp grated fresh root ginger
  5ml/1 tsp dark soy sauce
  1 garlic clove, crushed
  2.5ml/½ tsp sesame seeds
  5ml/1 tsp sesame oil
  ground black pepper
For the dipping sauce
  60ml/4 tbsp dark soy sauce
  10ml/2 tsp rice vinegar
  1 spring onion (scallion), chopped

1 Drain the mung beans and roll them between the palms of your hands to remove the skins. Rinse thoroughly, and place the peeled beans in a food processor with the pine nuts and 120ml/4fl oz/½ cup water. Blend well until they have formed a milky paste.

2 Transfer the bean paste to a bowl and add the rice four and 5ml/1 tsp salt. Mix well.

3 Put the beef into a large bowl. Pour over the mirin or rice wine for the marinade, then add the other marinade ingredients and mix well. Leave to marinate for 20 minutes. Season the prawns with salt and pepper.

4 Combine all the dipping sauce ingredients in a small serving bowl. Coat a frying pan or wok with vegetable oil and heat over medium heat.

5 Add the beef, mushroom and onion, and stir-fry until the meat has browned. Next, add the cucumber, cabbage and spring onions. Toss the ingredients in the pan and then remove from the heat.

6 Heat a little oil for shallow-frying in a frying pan and add a spoonful of the bean paste to form a small pancake. Spoon a little of the beef mixture on to the pancake, with some shredded chilli and a spoonful of chopped prawns. Use a metal spatula to press the mixture flat on to the pancake, and fry until golden on each side. Repeat until all the batter and beef mixture has been used up. Arrange the pancake fritters on a large serving platter and serve with the soy dipping sauce.

Energy 429Kcal/2070kJ; Protein 38.2g; Carbohydrate 55.4g, of which sugars 6.9g; Fat 14.2g, of which saturates 2.2g; Cholesterol 108mg; Calcium 175mg; Fibre 11.7g; Sodium 1867mg.

SPICED RED LENTIL AND COCONUT SOUP

HOT, SPICY AND RICHLY FLAVOURED, THIS SUBSTANTIAL SOUP IS ALMOST A MEAL IN ITSELF. IF YOU ARE REALLY HUNGRY, SERVE WITH CHUNKS OF WARMED NAAN BREAD OR THICK SLICES OF TOAST.

SERVES FOUR

INGREDIENTS
30ml/2 tbsp sunflower oil
2 red onions, finely chopped
1 birds' eye chilli, seeded and
   finely sliced
2 garlic cloves, chopped
2.5cm/1in piece fresh lemon grass,
   outer layers removed and inside
   finely sliced
200g/7oz/scant 1 cup red
   lentils, rinsed
5ml/1 tsp ground coriander
5ml/1 tsp paprika
400ml/14fl oz/1²/₃ cups
   coconut milk
900ml/1½ pints/3¾ cups water
juice of 1 lime
3 spring onions (scallions), chopped
20g/³/₄oz/scant 1 cup fresh coriander
   (cilantro), finely chopped
salt and ground black pepper

1 Heat the oil in a large pan and add the onions, chilli, garlic and lemon grass. Cook for 5 minutes or until the onions have softened but not browned, stirring occasionally.

2 Add the lentils and spices. Pour in the coconut milk and water, and stir until well mixed. Bring to the boil, stir, then reduce the heat and simmer for 40–45 minutes or until the lentils are soft and mushy.

3 Pour in the lime juice and add the spring onions and fresh coriander, reserving a little of each for the garnish. Season, then ladle into bowls. Garnish with the reserved spring onions and coriander.

Energy 263kcal/1109kJ; Protein 13.6g; Carbohydrate 39.5g, of which sugars 10.8g; Fat 6.8g, of which saturates 1g; Cholesterol 0mg; Calcium 96mg; Fibre 4.1g; Sodium 134mg.

LENTIL SOUP

THE SECRET OF A GOOD LENTIL SOUP IS TO BE GENEROUS WITH THE OLIVE OIL. THE SOUP IS SERVED AS A MAIN MEAL, ACCOMPANIED BY OLIVES, BREAD AND CHEESE.

SERVES FOUR

INGREDIENTS
275g/10oz/1¼ cups brown or green
  lentils, preferably the small variety
150ml/¼ pint/⅔ cup extra virgin
  olive oil
1 onion, thinly sliced
2 garlic cloves, sliced into
  thin batons
1 carrot, sliced into thin discs
400g/14oz can chopped tomatoes
15ml/1 tbsp tomato purée (paste)
2.5ml/½ tsp dried oregano
1 litre/1¾ pints/4 cups hot water
salt and ground black pepper
30ml/2 tbsp roughly chopped fresh
  herb leaves, to garnish

1 Rinse the lentils, drain them and put them in a large pan with cold water to cover. Bring to the boil and boil for 3–4 minutes. Strain, discarding the liquid, and set the lentils aside.

2 Wipe the pan clean, heat the olive oil in it, then add the onion and sauté until translucent. Stir in the garlic, then, as soon as it becomes aromatic, return the lentils to the pan. Add the carrot, tomatoes, tomato purée and oregano. Stir in the hot water and a little pepper to taste.

3 Bring to the boil, then lower the heat, cover the pan and cook gently for 20–30 minutes until the lentils feel soft but have not begun to disintegrate. Add salt and the chopped herbs just before serving.

Energy 463kcal/1937kJ; Protein 17.9g; Carbohydrate 40.4g, of which sugars 7.2g; Fat 26.7g, of which saturates 3.9g; Cholesterol 0mg; Calcium 67mg; Fibre 8g; Sodium 33mg.

MIXED BEAN SOUP

THIS CLASSIC VEGETARIAN SOUP, BETTER KNOWN AS PISTOU, HAS A MIXED BEAN BASE AND IS RICHLY FLAVOURED WITH A HOME-MADE GARLIC, FRESH BASIL AND PARMESAN PISTOU SAUCE.

SERVES FOUR TO SIX

INGREDIENTS

150g/5oz/scant 1 cup dried haricot (navy) beans, soaked overnight in cold water
150g/5oz/scant 1 cup dried flageolet or cannellini beans, soaked overnight in cold water
1 onion, chopped
1.2 litres/2 pints/5 cups hot vegetable stock
2 carrots, roughly chopped
225g/8oz Savoy cabbage, shredded
1 large potato, about 225g/8oz, roughly chopped
225g/8oz French (green) beans, chopped
salt and ground black pepper
basil leaves, to garnish
For the pistou
4 garlic cloves
8 large basil sprigs
90ml/6 tbsp olive oil
60ml/4 tbsp freshly grated Parmesan cheese

1 Soak a bean pot in cold water for 20 minutes then drain. If you don't have a bean pot use a large casserole dish, but there is not need to soak it. Drain the soaked haricot and flageolet or cannellini beans and place in the bean pot or casserole dish. Add the chopped onion and pour over sufficient cold water to come 5cm/2in above the beans. Cover and place the pot in an unheated oven. Set the oven to 200°C/400°F/Gas 6 and cook for about 1½ hours, or until the beans are tender.

2 Drain the beans and onions. Place half the beans and onions in a food processor or blender and process to a paste. Return the drained beans and the bean paste to the bean pot or casserole. Add the hot vegetable stock.

3 Add the chopped carrots, shredded cabbage, chopped potato and French beans to the bean pot or casserole. Season with salt and pepper, cover and return the pot to the oven. Reduce the oven temperature to 180°C/350°F/Gas 4 and cook for 1 hour, or until all the vegetables are cooked right through.

4 Meanwhile make the pistou: place the garlic and basil in a mortar and pound with a pestle, then gradually beat in the oil. Stir in the grated Parmesan. Stir half the pistou into the soup and then ladle it into warmed soup bowls. Top each bowl of soup with a spoonful of the remaining pistou and serve garnished with basil.

Energy 338kcal/1416kJ; Protein 17.2g; Carbohydrate 34.6g, of which sugars 7.5g; Fat 15.5g, of which saturates 3.8g; Cholesterol 10mg; Calcium 215mg; Fibre 10.8g; Sodium 133mg.

LENTIL AND PASTA SOUP

THIS RUSTIC VEGETARIAN SOUP MAKES A HEARTY AND WARMING WINTER MEAL AND GOES ESPECIALLY WELL WITH GRANARY OR CRUSTY ITALIAN BREAD.

SERVES FOUR TO SIX

INGREDIENTS

175g/6oz/³⁄₄ cup brown lentils
3 garlic cloves, unpeeled
1 litre/1³⁄₄ pints/4 cups water
45ml/3 tbsp olive oil
25g/1oz/2 tbsp butter
1 onion, finely chopped
2 celery sticks, finely chopped
30ml/2 tbsp sun-dried tomato
   purée (paste)
1.75 litres/3 pints/7¹⁄₂ cups
   vegetable stock
a few fresh marjoram leaves
a few fresh basil leaves
leaves from 1 fresh thyme sprig
50g/2oz/¹⁄₂ cup dried small pasta
   shapes, such as macaroni or tubetti
salt and ground black pepper
tiny fresh herb leaves, to garnish

1 Put the lentils in a large pan. Smash one of the garlic cloves using the blade of a large knife (there's no need to peel it first), then add it to the lentils. Pour in the water and bring to the boil. Simmer for about 20 minutes, or until the lentils are tender. Drain the lentils in a sieve, remove the garlic and set it aside. Rinse the lentils under the cold tap and leave to drain.

2 Heat 30ml/2 tbsp of the oil with half the butter in the pan. Add the onion and celery and cook gently for 5 minutes.

3 Crush the remaining garlic, then peel and mash the reserved garlic. Add to the pan with the remaining oil, the tomato purée and the lentils. Stir, then add the stock, herbs and salt and pepper. Bring to the boil, stirring. Simmer for 30 minutes, stirring occasionally.

4 Add the pasta and bring the soup back to the boil, stirring. Reduce the heat and simmer until the pasta is just tender. Add the remaining butter to the pan and stir until melted. Taste the soup for seasoning, then serve hot in warmed bowls, sprinkled with the fresh herb leaves.

Energy 179kcal/753kJ; Protein 8.4g; Carbohydrate 24.2g, of which sugars 2.3g; Fat 6.1g, of which saturates 0.9g; Cholesterol 0mg; Calcium 25mg; Fibre 2.1g; Sodium 29mg.

CANNELLINI BEAN SOUP

THIS SUBSTANTIAL BEAN SOUP IS SO POPULR IN GREECE THAT IT COULD ALMOST BE CALLED A NATIONAL FAVOURITE. IT IS ALWAYS SERVED WITH BREAD AND OLIVES, AND PERHAPS RAW ONION QUARTERS. IT HAS A HEARTY QUALITY AND FLAVOURFUL INGREDIENTS.

SERVES FOUR

INGREDIENTS

275g/10oz/1½ cups dried cannellini beans, soaked overnight in cold water
1 large onion, thinly sliced
1 celery stick, sliced
2–3 carrots, sliced in discs
400g/14oz can tomatoes
15ml/1 tbsp tomato purée (paste)
150ml/¼ pint/⅔ cup extra virgin olive oil
5ml/1 tsp dried oregano
30ml/2 tbsp finely chopped fresh flat leaf parsley
salt and ground black pepper

1 Drain the beans, rinse them under cold water and drain them again. Tip them into a large pan, pour in enough water to cover and bring to the boil. Cook for about 3 minutes, then drain.

2 Return the beans to the pan, pour in fresh water to cover them by about 3cm/1¼in, then add the onion, celery, carrots and tomatoes, and stir in the tomato purée, olive oil and oregano. Season with a little pepper, but don't add salt at this stage, as it would toughen the skins of the beans.

3 Bring to the boil, lower the heat and cook for about 1 hour, until the beans are just tender. Season with salt, stir in the parsley and serve.

Energy 460kcal/1922kJ; Protein 16.8g; Carbohydrate 41.1g, of which sugars 11.8g; Fat 26.5g, of which saturates 3.9g; Cholesterol 0mg; Calcium 103mg; Fibre 14g; Sodium 54mg.

CHICKPEA SOUP

COMPARED TO OTHER SOUPS BASED ON PULSES, WHICH ARE OFTEN VERY HEARTY, THIS HAS A UNIQUE LIGHTNESS IN TERMS OF BOTH FLAVOUR AND TEXTURE. WITH FRESH BREAD AND FETA CHEESE, IT MAKES A DELICIOUS, HEALTHY MEAL.

SERVES FOUR

INGREDIENTS
150ml/¼ pint/⅔ cup extra virgin
olive oil, plus extra for serving
1 large onion, chopped
350g/12oz/1¾ cups dried chickpeas,
soaked in cold water overnight
15ml/1 tbsp plain (all-purpose) flour
juice of 1 lemon, or more if needed
45ml/3 tbsp chopped fresh flat
leaf parsley
salt and ground black pepper

1 Heat the olive oil in a heavy pan, add the onion and sauté until it starts to colour. Meanwhile, drain the chickpeas, rinse them under cold water and drain them again. Shake the colander or sieve to dry the chickpeas as much as possible, then add them to the pan. Turn them with a spatula for a few minutes to coat them well in the oil, then pour in enough hot water to cover them by about 4cm/1½in.

2 Bring to the boil. Skim off any white froth that rises to the surface, using a slotted spoon. Lower the heat, add some pepper, cover and cook for 1–1¼ hours or until the chickpeas are soft.

3 Put the flour in a cup and stir in the lemon juice with a fork. When the chickpeas are perfectly soft, add this mixture to them. Mix well, then add salt and pepper to taste. Cover the pan and cook gently for 5–10 minutes more, stirring occasionally.

4 To thicken the soup slightly, take out about two cupfuls of the chickpeas and put them in a food processor. Process briefly so that the chickpeas are broken up, but remain slightly rough. Stir into the soup and mix well. Add the parsley, then taste the soup. If it seems a little bland, add more lemon juice. Serve in heated bowls and offer extra olive oil at the table, for drizzling on top of the soup.

Energy 557kcal/2330kJ; Protein 20.5g; Carbohydrate 54.5g, of which sugars 8.2g; Fat 30.1g, of which saturates 4g; Cholesterol 0mg; Calcium 193mg; Fibre 11.5g; Sodium 41mg.

BRAISED BEAN AND WHEAT SOUP

THIS DISH IS WONDERFULLY EASY TO MAKE, BUT IT IS VITAL THAT YOU START SOAKING THE PULSES AND WHEAT THE DAY BEFORE YOU WANT TO SERVE IT. OFFER SOME TASTY EXTRA VIRGIN OLIVE OIL AT THE TABLE, SO GUESTS CAN DRIZZLE A LITTLE OIL OVER THEIR FOOD.

SERVES FOUR

INGREDIENTS

200g/7oz/1¼ cups mixed beans
  and lentils
25g/1oz/2 tbsp whole wheat grains
150ml/¼ pint/⅔ cup extra virgin
  olive oil
1 large onion, finely chopped
2 garlic cloves, crushed
5–6 fresh sage leaves, chopped
juice of 1 lemon
3 spring onions (scallions),
  thinly sliced
60–75ml/4–5 tbsp chopped fresh dill
salt and ground black pepper

1 Put the pulses and wheat in a large bowl and cover with cold water. Leave to soak overnight.

2 Next day, drain the pulse mixture, rinse it under cold water and drain again. Put the mixture in a large pan. Cover with plenty of cold water and cook for about 1½ hours, by which time all the ingredients will be quite soft. Strain, reserving 475ml/16fl oz/2 cups of the cooking liquid. Return the bean mixture to the clean pan.

3 Heat the oil in a frying pan and fry the onion until light golden. Add the garlic and sage. As soon as the garlic becomes aromatic, add the mixture to the beans. Stir in the reserved liquid, add plenty of seasoning and simmer for about 15 minutes, or until the pulses are piping hot. Stir in the lemon juice, then spoon into serving bowls, top with a sprinkling of spring onions and dill and serve.

Energy 442kcal/1844kJ; Protein 14.1g; Carbohydrate 39.2g, of which sugars 5.9g; Fat 26.5g, of which saturates 3.7g; Cholesterol 0mg; Calcium 76mg; Fibre 4.7g; Sodium 27mg.

BEAN RIBOLLITA

ORIGINATING FROM TUSCANY, THE NAME RIBOLLITA OR "RE-BOILED" DERIVES FROM THE FACT THAT THE SOUP TASTES BETTER THE DAY AFTER IT HAS BEEN MADE. TRADITIONALLY IT IS SERVED LADLED OVER BREAD AND A DARK GREEN VEGETABLE, ALTHOUGH YOU COULD OMIT THIS FOR A LIGHTER VERSION.

SERVES SIX TO EIGHT

INGREDIENTS
  45ml/3 tbsp olive oil
  2 onions, chopped
  2 carrots, sliced
  4 garlic cloves, crushed
  2 celery sticks, thinly sliced
  1 fennel bulb, trimmed and chopped
  2 large courgettes (zucchini),
    thinly sliced
  400g/14oz can chopped tomatoes
  30ml/2 tbsp home-made or
    bought pesto
  900ml/1½ pints/3¾ cups
    vegetable stock
  400g/14oz can haricot (navy) or
    borlotti beans, drained
  salt and ground black pepper
To serve
  450g/1lb young spinach
  15ml/1 tbsp extra virgin olive oil,
    plus extra for drizzling
  6–8 slices white bread
  Parmesan cheese shavings

1 Heat the oil in a large pan. Add the onions, carrots, garlic, celery and fennel, and fry gently for 10 minutes. Add the courgettes and fry for a further 2 minutes.

VARIATION
Use other beans such as chickpeas or cannellini, or dark greens, such as chard or cabbage, instead of the spinach.

2 Add the chopped tomatoes, pesto, stock and beans, and bring to the boil. Reduce the heat, cover and simmer gently for 25–30 minutes, until the vegetables are completely tender. Season with salt and pepper to taste.

3 To serve, fry the spinach in the oil for 2 minutes or until wilted. Spoon over the bread in soup bowls, then ladle the soup over the spinach. Serve with extra olive oil for drizzling on to the soup and Parmesan cheese to sprinkle on top.

Energy 227kcal/952kJ; Protein 10.5g; Carbohydrate 28.9g, of which sugars 11.2g; Fat 8.5g, of which saturates 1.8g; Cholesterol 4mg; Calcium 245mg; Fibre 7.9g; Sodium 444mg.

MEAT, BEAN AND LENTIL SOUP

THIS IS A HEARTY MEAT, BEAN AND LENTIL SOUP, KNOWN AS HARIRA, AND TRADITIONAL TO MOROCCO. THE LAMB AND LENTILS ARE SIMMERED GENTLY WITH WARMING SPICES.

SERVES FOUR

INGREDIENTS
  450g/1lb well-flavoured tomatoes
  225g/8oz lamb, cut into
    1cm/1/2in pieces
  2.5ml/1/2 tsp ground turmeric
  2.5ml/1/2 tsp ground cinnamon
  25g/1oz/2 tbsp butter
  60ml/4 tbsp chopped fresh
    coriander (cilantro)
  30ml/2 tbsp chopped fresh parsley
  1 onion, chopped
  50g/2oz/1/4 cup split red lentils
  75g/3oz/1/2 cup dried chickpeas,
    soaked overnight and drained
  4 baby onions or small
    shallots, peeled
  25g/1oz/1/4 cup soup noodles
salt and ground black pepper
chopped fresh coriander (cilantro),
  lemon slices and ground cinnamon,
  to garnish

1 Plunge the tomatoes into boiling water for 30 seconds, then rinse in cold water. Peel, seed and roughly chop.

2 Put the lamb, turmeric, cinnamon, butter, coriander, parsley and onion into a large pan, and cook over a moderate heat, stirring, for 5 minutes. Add the chopped tomatoes and continue to cook for 10 minutes.

3 Rinse the lentils and add to the pan with the chickpeas and 600ml/1 pint/2½ cups water. Bring to the boil, cover, and simmer gently for 1 hour. Add the baby onions and continue to cook for a further 30 minutes

4 Add the soup noodles about 5 minutes before the end of the cooking time. Season to taste. Garnish with the coriander, lemon slices and cinnamon.

Energy 297kcal/1248kJ; Protein 19.6g; Carbohydrate 26.4g, of which sugars 5.4g; Fat 13.1g, of which saturates 6.4g; Cholesterol 56mg; Calcium 75mg; Fibre 4.5g; Sodium 113mg.

SPICY PEANUT SOUP

*THIS DISTINCTIVE SOUP IS MADE WITH AN UNUSUAL COMBINATION OF INGREDIENTS. IT HAS A RICH
PEANUT AND CHILLI FLAVOUR AND A THICK TEXTURE MAKING IT A GOOD FILLING AUTUMNAL CHOICE.*

SERVES SIX

INGREDIENTS

  30ml/2 tbsp oil
  1 large onion, finely chopped
  2 garlic cloves, crushed
  5ml/1 tsp mild chilli powder
  2 red (bell) peppers, seeded and
    finely chopped
  225g/8oz carrots, finely chopped
  225g/8oz potatoes, peeled and cubed
  3 celery sticks, sliced
  900ml/1½ pints/3¾ cups
    vegetable stock
  90ml/6 tbsp crunchy peanut butter
  115g/4oz/²⁄₃ cup corn
  salt and ground black pepper
  roughly chopped unsalted roasted
    peanuts, to garnish

1 Heat the oil in a large pan and
cook the onion and garlic for about
3 minutes. Add the chilli powder and
cook for a further 1 minute.

2 Add the peppers, carrots, potatoes
and celery to the pan. Stir well,
then cook for a further 4 minutes,
stirring occasionally.

3 Stir in the stock, peanut butter and
corn until combined.

4 Season well. Bring to the boil,
cover and simmer for 20 minutes, or
until all the vegetables are tender.
Adjust the seasoning before serving,
and sprinkle with the chopped roasted
peanuts, to garnish.

Energy 222kcal/925kJ; Protein 6g; Carbohydrate 23.4g, of which sugars 12.1g; Fat 12.2g, of which saturates 2.6g; Cholesterol 0mg; Calcium 41mg; Fibre 4g; Sodium 130mg.

BLACK-EYE BEAN SOUP

This delicious Israeli black-eyed bean and turmeric-tinted tomato broth, is flavoured with tangy lemon and speckled with chopped fresh coriander. It's a filling soup that is ideal for lunch or served as a light supper dish.

SERVES FOUR

INGREDIENTS

175g/6oz/1 cup black-eyed
  beans (peas)
15ml/1 tbsp olive oil
2 onions, chopped
4 garlic cloves, chopped
1 medium-hot or 2–3 mild fresh
  chillies, chopped
5ml/1 tsp ground cumin
5ml/1 tsp ground turmeric
250g/9oz fresh or canned
  tomatoes, diced
600ml/1 pint/2½ cups chicken,
  beef or vegetable stock
25g/1oz fresh coriander (cilantro)
  leaves, roughly chopped
juice of ½ lemon
pitta bread, to serve

1 Put the beans in a pan, cover with cold water, bring to the boil, then cook for 5 minutes. Remove from the heat, cover and leave to stand for 2 hours.

2 Heat the oil in a pan, add the onions, garlic and chilli and cook for 5 minutes, or until the onion is soft. Stir in the cumin, turmeric, tomatoes, stock, half the coriander and the beans and simmer for 20–30 minutes. Stir in the lemon juice and remaining coriander and serve at once with pitta bread.

Energy 167kcal/706kJ; Protein 10.9g; Carbohydrate 24g, of which sugars 5g; Fat 3.8g, of which saturates 0.6g; Cholesterol 0mg; Calcium 81mg; Fibre 8.6g; Sodium 19mg.

BEAN AND HOCK SOUP

THIS CLASSIC GALICIAN SOUP FEATURES SALT PORK AND HARICOT BEANS WITH YOUNG TURNIPS.
GALICIA IS A REGION IN THE NORTH-WEST CORNER OF SPAIN AND IS RENOWNED FOR ITS HEARTY FARE.
YOU WILL NEED TO START MAKING THE SOUP AT LEAST A DAY IN ADVANCE.

SERVES SIX

INGREDIENTS
  150g/5oz/⅔ cup haricot (navy) beans,
    soaked overnight in cold water
    and drained
  1kg/2¼lb smoked gammon (cured
    or smoked ham) hock
  3 potatoes, quartered
  3 small turnips, sliced in rounds
  150g/5oz purple sprouting broccoli
  salt and ground black pepper

1 Put the drained beans and gammon
into a flameproof casserole and cover
with 2 litres/3½ pints/8 cups water.
Slowly bring to the boil, skim off any
scum, then turn down the heat and
cook gently, covered, for about 1¼ hours.

2 Drain, reserving the broth. Return the
broth to the casserole and add the
potatoes, turnips and drained beans.

3 Meanwhile, strip all the gammon off
the bone and return the bone to the
broth. Discard the rind, fat and gristle
and chop half the meat coarsely. Reserve
the remaining meat for another recipe.

4 Add the chopped meat to the
casserole. Discard the hard stalks from
the broccoli and add the leaves and florets
to the broth. Simmer for 10 minutes.
Season generously with pepper, then
remove the bone and leave the soup to
stand for at least half a day.

5 To serve, reheat the soup, add a little
more seasoning if necessary, and ladle
into soup bowls.

COOK'S TIP
The leftover gammon can be chopped
into bitesize pieces and added to rice or
vegetable dishes, or tortillas.

Energy 242kcal/1020kJ; Protein 22.6g; Carbohydrate 23.4g, of which sugars 3g; Fat 7.1g, of which saturates 2.3g; Cholesterol 19mg; Calcium 61mg; Fibre 5.8g; Sodium 751mg.

PASTA AND CHICKPEA SOUP

A SIMPLE, COUNTRY-STYLE SOUP. THE SHAPES OF THE PASTA AND THE BEANS COMPLEMENT ONE ANOTHER BEAUTIFULLY. LOOK OUT FOR REALLY LARGE PASTA SHELLS.

SERVES FOUR TO SIX

INGREDIENTS

1 onion
2 carrots
2 celery sticks
60ml/4 tbsp olive oil
400g/14oz chickpeas, rinsed
  and drained
200g/7oz can cannellini beans,
  rinsed and drained
150ml/¼ pint/⅔ cup passata
  (bottled strained tomatoes)
120ml/4fl oz/½ cup water
1.5 litres/2½ pints/6¼ cups
  chicken stock
2 fresh or dried rosemary sprigs
200g/7oz dried giant conchiglie
sea salt and ground black pepper
freshly grated Parmesan cheese,
  to serve

1 Chop the onion, carrots and celery sticks finely, either in a food processor or by hand.

2 Heat the olive oil in a large pan, add the chopped vegetable mixture and cook over a low heat, stirring frequently, for 5 minutes, or until the vegetables are just beginning to soften.

3 Add the chickpeas and cannellini beans, stir well to mix, then cook for 5 minutes. Stir in the passata and water, then cook, stirring for 2–3 minutes.

4 Add 475ml/16fl oz/2 cups of the stock and one of the rosemary sprigs. Bring to the boil, cover, then simmer gently, stirring occasionally, for 1 hour.

5 Pour in the remaining stock, add the pasta and bring to boil, stirring. Lower the heat slightly and simmer, stirring frequently, until the pasta is al dente: 7–8 minutes or according to the instructions on the packet.

6 When the pasta is cooked, taste the soup for seasoning. Remove the rosemary and serve the soup hot in warmed bowls, topped with grated cheese and a few rosemary leaves from the rosemary sprig.

Energy 270kcal/1139kJ; Protein 9.3g; Carbohydrate 38.4g, of which sugars 4g; Fat 10g, of which saturates 1.3g; Cholesterol 0mg; Calcium 50mg; Fibre 4.5g; Sodium 216mg.

YELLOW PEA SOUP

SWEET AND MILD IN FLAVOUR, YELLOW SPLIT PEAS ARE SOLD DRIED AND SPLIT IN HALF. THIS IS A FILLING SOUP THAT COULD BE SERVED AS A MAIN COURSE.

SERVES SIX TO EIGHT

INGREDIENTS
500g/1¼lb yellow split peas
30ml/2 tbsp vegetable oil
1 Spanish (Bermuda) onion, sliced
500g/1¼lb salted pork belly
  or bacon
2 litres/3½ pints/8 cups water or
  ham stock
bay leaf
1 bunch thyme sprigs
5ml/1 tsp chopped fresh thyme
  and/or marjoram
salt
mustard, to serve

1 Soak the yellow split peas in cold water overnight. The next day, drain them and put to one side.

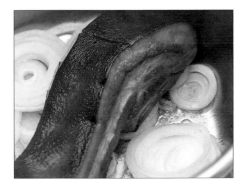

2 Heat the oil in a large, heavy pan, add the onion and pork belly and when browned, add the water or ham stock. Heat until simmering then skim off any foam and cook for about 1 hour.

3 Add the peas, bay leaf and thyme sprigs and leave to cook for about a further hour until the peas are soft and the pork is cooked and falling apart.

4 Remove the pork from the pan and cut it into cubes, then return it to the pan with the fresh thyme and/or marjoram.

5 Season the soup with salt to taste before serving, although because the meat is salty it may not need extra seasoning. Serve with the mustard and a hard bread such as polar flat bread.

Energy 374Kcal/1569kJ; Protein 25.8g; Carbohydrate 38.3g, of which sugars 3.7g; Fat 14g, of which saturates 4.3g; Cholesterol 33mg; Calcium 57mg; Fibre 3.9g; Sodium 988mg.

SALADS AND SIDE DISHES

Beans and lentils are classic accompaniments to a wide variety of main meals, as well as the basis for salads. These foods readily absorb the flavour of other ingredients, such as herbs and spices, and provide satisfying side dishes that complement a whole range of fish, poultry, meat and vegetarian courses. They are complex carbohydrates, so offer a filling and nutritious addition to a meal.

WHITE BEAN SALAD <small>WITH</small> RED PEPPER DRESSING

THE SPECKLED HERB AND RED PEPPER DRESSING ADDS A WONDERFUL COLOUR CONTRAST TO THIS SALAD, WHICH IS BEST SERVED WARM. CANNED BEANS ARE USED FOR CONVENIENCE.

SERVES FOUR

INGREDIENTS

  1 large red (bell) pepper
  60ml/4 tbsp olive oil
  1 large garlic clove, crushed
  25g/1oz/1 cup fresh oregano leaves
    or flat leaf parsley
  15ml/1 tbsp balsamic vinegar
  2 x 400g/14oz/3 cups cans flageolet
    beans, drained and rinsed
  400g/14oz can cannellini beans,
    drained and rinsed
  salt and ground black pepper

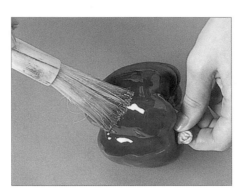

1 Preheat the oven to 200°C/400°F/ Gas 6. Place the red pepper on a baking sheet, brush with oil and roast for 30 minutes or until the skin wrinkles and the flesh is soft.

2 Remove the pepper from the oven and place in a plastic bag. Seal and leave to cool. (This makes the skin easier to remove.)

3 When the pepper is cool enough to handle, remove it from the bag and peel off the skin. Rinse under cold running water. Slice the pepper in half, remove the seeds and dice. Set aside.

4 Heat the remaining oil in a pan and cook the garlic for 1 minute until softened. Remove from the heat, then add the oregano or parsley, the red pepper and any juices, and the balsamic vinegar.

5 Put the beans in a large bowl and pour over the dressing. Season to taste, then stir gently until combined. Serve warm.

Energy 267kcal/1117kJ; Protein 11.1g; Carbohydrate 29.8g, of which sugars 8.3g; Fat 12.2g, of which saturates 1.8g; Cholesterol 0mg; Calcium 133mg; Fibre 10.6g; Sodium 591mg.

BEAN SALAD WITH TUNA AND RED ONION

THIS TASTY SALAD MAKES A GREAT LIGHT MAIN MEAL IF SERVED WITH A GREEN SALAD, SOME GARLIC MAYONNAISE AND PLENTY OF WARM, CRUSTY BREAD.

SERVES FOUR

INGREDIENTS
250g/9oz/1⅓ cups dried haricot (navy) or cannellini beans, soaked overnight in cold water
1 bay leaf
200–250g/7–9oz fine French (green) beans, trimmed
1 large red onion, very thinly sliced
45ml/3 tbsp chopped fresh flat leaf parsley
200g/7oz can good-quality tuna in olive oil, drained
200g/7oz cherry tomatoes, halved
salt and ground black pepper
a few onion rings, to garnish
For the dressing
90ml/6 tbsp extra virgin olive oil
15ml/1 tbsp tarragon vinegar
5ml/1 tsp tarragon mustard
1 garlic clove, finely chopped
5ml/1 tsp grated lemon rind
a little lemon juice
pinch of caster (superfine) sugar

1 Drain the beans and bring them to the boil in fresh water with the bay leaf added. Boil rapidly for 10 minutes, then reduce the heat and boil steadily for 1–1½ hours, until tender. Drain well. Discard the bay leaf.

3 Blanch the French beans in plenty of boiling water for 3–4 minutes. Drain, refresh under cold water and drain thoroughly again.

5 Flake the tuna into large chunks with a knife and toss it into the beans with the tomato halves.

6 Arrange the salad on four individual plates. Drizzle the remaining dressing over the salad and scatter the remaining chopped parsley on top. Garnish with a few onion rings and serve immediately, at room temperature.

2 Meanwhile, place all the dressing ingredients apart from the lemon juice and sugar in a jug and whisk until mixed. Season and add the lemon juice and a pinch of caster sugar, if liked.

4 Place both types of beans in a bowl. Add half the dressing and toss to mix. Stir in the onion and half the chopped parsley, then season to taste with salt and pepper.

Energy 434kcal/1817kJ; Protein 29g; Carbohydrate 31g, of which sugars 4.5g; Fat 22.4g, of which saturates 3.3g; Cholesterol 25mg; Calcium 113mg; Fibre 12g; Sodium 165mg.

BROWN BEAN SALAD

BROWN BEANS, SOMETIMES CALLED FUL MEDAMES, ARE AVAILABLE FROM HEALTH-FOOD SHOPS AND MIDDLE EASTERN GROCERY STORES. DRIED BROAD BEANS OR BLACK OR RED KIDNEY BEANS MAKE A GOOD SUBSTITUTE. THIS IS A FILLING, HEALTHY AND NUTRITIOUS LUNCH TIME SALAD.

SERVES SIX

INGREDIENTS

350g/12oz/1½ cups dried
  brown beans
3 fresh thyme sprigs
2 bay leaves
1 onion, halved
4 garlic cloves, crushed
7.5ml/1½ tsp crushed cumin seeds
3 spring onions (scallions), chopped
90ml/6 tbsp chopped fresh parsley
20ml/4 tsp lemon juice
90ml/6 tbsp olive oil
3 hard-boiled eggs, roughly chopped
1 gherkin, roughly chopped
salt and ground black pepper

COOK'S TIP
The cooking time for the brown beans may vary depending on the age of the beans – the older they are, the longer they take.

1 Put the beans in a bowl with plenty of cold water and leave to soak overnight. Drain, transfer to a pan and cover with fresh water. Bring to the boil and boil rapidly for 10 minutes.

2 Reduce the heat and add the thyme, bay leaves and onion. Simmer very gently for about 1 hour, until tender. Drain and discard the herbs and onion.

3 Place the beans in a large bowl. Mix together the garlic, cumin seeds, spring onions, parsley, lemon juice and oil in a small bowl, and add a little salt and pepper. Pour over the beans and toss the ingredients lightly together.

4 Gently stir in the eggs and gherkin. Transfer the salad to a serving dish and serve at once.

Energy 355kcal/1488kJ; Protein 19.5g; Carbohydrate 32g, of which sugars 2.6g; Fat 17.6g, of which saturates 3g; Cholesterol 114mg; Calcium 92mg; Fibre 11.2g; Sodium 55mg.

PEPPERY BEAN SALAD

THIS VIBRANT SALAD USES CANNED BEANS FOR SPEED AND CONVENIENCE. TRY VARYING THE SELECTION OF BEANS ACCORDING TO WHAT YOU HAVE TO HAND OR PERSONAL PREFERENCE.

SERVES FOUR TO SIX

INGREDIENTS
    425g/15oz can red kidney beans
    425g/15oz can black-eyed beans (peas)
    425g/15oz can chickpeas
    ¼ red (bell) pepper
    ¼ green (bell) pepper
    6 radishes
    15ml/1 tbsp sliced spring onion
      (scallion), to garnish
    salt
For the dressing
    5ml/1 tsp ground cumin
    15ml/1 tbsp tomato ketchup
    30ml/2 tbsp olive oil
    15ml/1 tbsp white wine vinegar
    1 garlic clove, crushed
    2.5ml/½ tsp hot pepper sauce

1 Rinse and drain the red kidney beans, black-eyed beans and chickpeas. Turn them into a large bowl.

2 Core, seed and chop the red and green peppers. Trim the radishes and slice thinly. Add the peppers, radishes and spring onion to the beans.

3 Mix together the cumin, ketchup, oil, vinegar and garlic in a small bowl. Add a little salt and hot pepper sauce to taste and stir again thoroughly.

4 Pour the dressing over the salad and mix. Chill the salad for at least 1 hour before serving, garnished with the sliced spring onion.

Energy 243kcal/1025kJ; Protein 14.1g; Carbohydrate 37.6g, of which sugars 9.1g; Fat 5g, of which saturates 0.8g; Cholesterol 0mg; Calcium 146mg; Fibre 12.8g; Sodium 823mg.

Tofu and Cucumber Salad

A NUTRITIOUS AND REFRESHING SALAD WITH A CHILLI-SPIKED, SWEET-AND-SOUR DRESSING, WHICH GOES PARTICULARLY WELL WITH THE MILD TASTING TOFU AND CRISP VEGETABLES.

SERVES FOUR TO SIX

INGREDIENTS
  1 small cucumber
  115g/4oz tofu
  oil, for frying
  115g/4oz/½ cup beansprouts
  salt
  celery leaves, to garnish
For the dressing
  1 small onion, grated
  2 garlic cloves, crushed
  5–7.5ml/1–1½ tsp chilli sauce
  30–45ml/2–3 tbsp dark soy sauce
  15–30ml/1–2 tbsp rice vinegar
  10ml/2 tsp dark brown sugar

1 Cut the cucumber into neat cubes. Sprinkle with salt to extract excess liquid. Set aside, while preparing the remaining ingredients.

2 Cut the tofu into cubes. Heat a little oil in a pan and fry on both sides until golden brown. Drain on kitchen paper.

3 To make the dressing, shake together the onion, garlic and chilli sauce in a screw-top jar. Add the soy sauce, vinegar, sugar and salt to taste.

4 Just before serving, rinse the cucumber under cold running water. Drain and dry thoroughly. Toss the cucumber, tofu and beansprouts together in a serving bowl and pour over the dressing. Garnish with the celery leaves and serve the salad at once.

Energy 30kcal/125kJ; Protein 2.7g; Carbohydrate 2.8g, of which sugars 2.1g; Fat 1g, of which saturates 0.1g; Cholesterol 0mg; Calcium 111mg; Fibre 0.6g; Sodium 537mg.

PUY LENTIL AND CABBAGE SALAD

THIS WARM, CRUNCHY SALAD MAKES A SATISFYING AND NUTRITIOUS MEAL IF SERVED WITH CRUSTY FRENCH BREAD OR WHOLEMEAL ROLLS.

SERVES FOUR TO SIX

INGREDIENTS

225g/8oz/1 cup puy lentils
1.5 litres/2½ pints/6¼ cups water
3 garlic cloves
1 bay leaf
1 small onion, peeled and studded
  with 2 cloves
15ml/1 tbsp olive oil
1 red onion, finely sliced
15ml/1 tbsp fresh thyme leaves
350g/12oz cabbage, finely shredded
finely grated rind and juice of
  1 lemon
15ml/1 tbsp raspberry vinegar
salt and ground black pepper

1 Rinse the lentils in cold water and place in a large pan with the water, one of the garlic cloves, the bay leaf and clove-studded onion. Bring to the boil and cook for 10 minutes. Reduce the heat, cover and simmer gently for 15–20 minutes. Drain and discard the onion, garlic and bay leaf.

2 Crush the remaining garlic cloves. Heat the oil in a large pan. Add the red onion, crushed garlic and thyme and cook for 5 minutes, until softened.

3 Add the cabbage and cook for 3–5 minutes, until just cooked but still crunchy.

4 Stir in the cooked lentils, lemon rind and juice and the raspberry vinegar. Season to taste and serve warm.

Energy 147kcal/623kJ; Protein 10.1g; Carbohydrate 22g, of which sugars 3.9g; Fat 2.7g, of which saturates 0.3g; Cholesterol 0mg; Calcium 58mg; Fibre 4.7g; Sodium 9mg.

BEANSPROUT AND DAIKON SALAD

RIBBON-THIN SLICES OF FRESH, CRISP VEGETABLES, EACH WITH THEIR OWN DISTINCT FLAVOUR,
MIXED WITH BEANSPROUTS, WHICH HAVE A CRUNCHY TEXTURE MAKE THE PERFECT FOIL FOR
AN UNUSUAL ORIENTAL DRESSING.

2 Wash the beansprouts and drain thoroughly in a colander.

3 Peel the cucumber, cut in half lengthways. Scoop out the seeds. Peel the cucumber flesh into long ribbon strips using a potato peeler.

4 Peel the carrots and radish into long ribbon strips in the same way as the cucumber.

5 Place the carrots, radish and cucumber in a large, shallow serving dish, add the onion, ginger, chilli and coriander or mint and toss to mix. Pour the dressing over just before serving.

SERVES FOUR

INGREDIENTS
    225g/8oz/1 cup beansprouts
    1 cucumber
    2 carrots
    1 small daikon radish
    1 small red onion, thinly sliced
    2.5cm/1in fresh root ginger, peeled
      and cut into thin matchsticks
    1 small red chilli, seeded and
      thinly sliced
    handful of fresh coriander (cilantro)
      or mint leaves
For the dressing
    15ml/1 tbsp rice vinegar
    15ml/1 tbsp light soy sauce
    15ml/1 tbsp Thai fish sauce
    1 garlic clove, finely chopped
    15ml/1 tbsp sesame oil
    45ml/3 tbsp groundnut oil
    30ml/2 tbsp sesame seeds,
      lightly toasted

1 First make the dressing. Place all the dressing ingredients in a bottle or screw-top jar and shake well. The dressing may be made in advance and will keep well for a couple of days if stored in the refrigerator or a cool place.

Energy 185kcal/766kJ; Protein 3.9g; Carbohydrate 7.3g, of which sugars 5.7g; Fat 15.8g, of which saturates 2.1g; Cholesterol 0mg; Calcium 79mg; Fibre 2.6g; Sodium 547mg.

LENTIL SALAD <u>WITH</u> RED ONIONS <u>AND</u> GARLIC

THIS DELICIOUS, GARLICKY LENTIL SALAD CAN BE SERVED WARM OR COLD AS AN ACCOMPANIMENT TO CHICKEN, MEAT, FISH OR VEGETABLE DISHES, AS AN APPETIZER OR A SALAD IN ITS OWN RIGHT. SERVE THE SALAD WITH A GENEROUS SPOONFUL OF PLAIN YOGURT.

SERVES FOUR

INGREDIENTS

  45ml/3 tbsp olive oil
  2 red onions, chopped
  2 tomatoes, peeled, seeded
   and chopped
  10ml/2 tsp ground turmeric
  10ml/2 tsp ground cumin
  175g/6oz/¾ cup brown or green
   lentils, picked over and rinsed
  900ml/1½ pints/3¾ cups vegetable
   stock or water
  4 garlic cloves, crushed
  small bunch of fresh coriander
   (cilantro), finely chopped
  salt and ground black pepper
  1 lemon, cut into wedges, to serve

1 Heat 30ml/2 tbsp of the oil in a large pan or flameproof casserole and fry the onions until soft. Add the tomatoes, turmeric and cumin, then stir in the lentils.

2 Pour in the stock or water and bring to the boil, then reduce the heat and simmer until the lentils are tender and almost all the liquid has been absorbed.

3 In a separate pan, fry the garlic in the remaining oil until golden brown. Toss the garlic into the lentils with the fresh coriander and season to taste. Serve warm or at room temperature, with wedges of lemon for squeezing juice over to taste.

VARIATION
If you prefer, you can replace the lentils with mung beans – they work just as well.

Energy 244kcal/1025kJ; Protein 12.3g; Carbohydrate 29.2g, of which sugars 6.6g; Fat 9.5g, of which saturates 1.3g; Cholesterol 0mg; Calcium 78mg; Fibre 6.1g; Sodium 16mg.

SPLIT PEA AND SHALLOT MASH

THIS PURÉE MAKES AN EXCELLENT ALTERNATIVE TO MASHED POTATOES, AND IS PARTICULARLY GOOD WITH WINTER PIES AND NUT ROASTS. IT CAN ALSO BE SERVED WITH WARMED PITTA BREAD.

2 Place the peas in a pan, cover with fresh cold water and bring to the boil. Skim off any foam that rises to the surface, then reduce the heat. Add the bay leaf and sage, and simmer for 30–40 minutes until the peas are tender. Add more water during cooking, if necessary.

3 Meanwhile, heat the oil in a frying pan and cook the shallots, cumin seeds and garlic for 3 minutes or until the shallots soften, stirring occasionally. Add the mixture to the split peas while they are still cooking.

4 Drain the split peas, reserving the cooking water. Remove the bay leaf, then place the split peas in a food processor or blender with the butter and season well.

5 Add 105ml/7 tbsp of the reserved cooking water and blend until the mixture forms a coarse purée. Add more water if the mash seems to be too dry. Adjust the seasoning and serve warm.

SERVES FOUR TO SIX

INGREDIENTS
  225g/8oz/1 cup yellow split peas
  1 bay leaf
  8 sage leaves, roughly chopped
  15ml/1 tbsp olive oil
  3 shallots, finely chopped
  heaped 1 tsp cumin seeds
  1 large garlic clove, chopped
  50g/2oz/4 tbsp butter, softened
  salt and ground black pepper

1 Place the split peas in a bowl and cover with cold water. Leave to soak overnight, then rinse and drain.

COOK'S TIP
Cannellini beans would make a good alternative to the yellow split peas. Soak overnight then drain and rinse. Cover the beans with fresh water and cook for about 1 hour or until tender.

Energy 201kcal/845kJ; Protein 9.1g; Carbohydrate 22g, of which sugars 1.5g; Fat 9.2g, of which saturates 4.7g; Cholesterol 18mg; Calcium 23mg; Fibre 2g; Sodium 64mg.

COURGETTES AND TOFU WITH TOMATO SAUCE

THIS MEDITERRANEAN-STYLE DISH IS GREAT HOT OR COLD, AND IMPROVES GIVEN A DAY OR TWO COVERED IN THE REFRIGERATOR. IT MAKES THE PERFECT ACCOMPANIMENT TO A NUT OR MEAT ROAST.

SERVES FOUR

INGREDIENTS
    30ml/2 tbsp olive oil
    2 garlic cloves, finely chopped
    4 large courgettes (zucchini), thinly
       sliced on the diagonal
    250g/9oz firm tofu, drained
       and cubed
    1 lemon
    sea salt and ground black pepper
For the tomato sauce
    10ml/2 tsp balsamic vinegar
    5ml/1 tsp sugar
    300ml/½ pint/1¼ cups passata
       (bottled strained tomatoes)
    small bunch of fresh mint, chopped

3 Add the tofu to the pan and brown for a few minutes. Turn gently, then brown again. Grate the rind from half the lemon and reserve for the garnish. Squeeze the lemon juice over the tofu.

4 Season to taste with sea salt and pepper, then leave to sizzle until all the lemon juice has evaporated. Gently stir the courgettes into the tofu until well combined, then remove the pan from the heat.

5 Transfer the courgettes and tofu to a warm serving dish and pour the tomato sauce over the top. Sprinkle with the grated lemon rind. Taste and season with more salt and pepper, if necessary, and serve immediately.

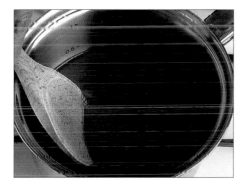

1 First, make the tomato sauce, Place all the ingredients in a small pan and heat through gently, stirring occasionally.

2 Meanwhile, heat the olive oil in a large non-stick frying pan until very hot, then add the garlic and stir-fry for 30 seconds, until golden. Add the courgettes and stir-fry over a high heat for about 5–6 minutes, or until the slices are golden around the edges. Remove from the pan.

VARIATIONS
• The courgette slices could be grilled (broiled) and then added to the fried garlic before the tofu cubes are browned.
• Aubergine (eggplant) slices could be used instead of the courgettes, but more olive oil may be needed to fry them in step 2.

Energy 141kcal/585kJ; Protein 8.8g; Carbohydrate 6.8g, of which sugars 6.3g; Fat 8.9g, of which saturates 1.3g; Cholesterol 0mg; Calcium 389mg; Fibre 2.4g; Sodium 181mg.

SPICY TAMARIND CHICKPEAS

CHICKPEAS MAKE A GOOD BASE FOR MANY VEGETARIAN DISHES. HERE, THEY ARE TOSSED WITH SOUR TAMARIND AND AROMATIC SPICES TO MAKE A DELICIOUSLY LIGHT MEAT-FREE LUNCH OR SIDE DISH.

SERVES FOUR

INGREDIENTS

225g/8oz/1¼ cups dried chickpeas
900ml/1½ pints/3½ cups
  boiling water
50g/2oz tamarind pulp
45ml/3 tbsp vegetable oil
2.5ml/½ tsp cumin seeds
1 onion, very finely chopped
2 garlic cloves, crushed
2.5cm/1in piece fresh root ginger,
  peeled and grated
5ml/1 tsp ground cumin
5ml/1 tsp ground coriander
1.5ml/¼ tsp ground turmeric
1 fresh green chilli, finely chopped
2.5ml/½ tsp salt
225g/8oz tomatoes, peeled and
  finely chopped
2.5ml/½ tsp garam masala
chopped fresh chillies and chopped
  onion, to garnish

1 Put the chickpeas in a large bowl and pour over cold water to cover. Leave to soak for at least 8 hours, or overnight.

2 Drain the chickpeas and put in a pan with at least double their volume of cold water. (Do not add salt to the water because this will toughen the chickpeas and spoil the final dish.)

3 Bring the water to the boil and boil vigorously for at least 10 minutes. Skim off any scum, then drain the chickpeas and tip into a large pan.

4 Pour 750ml/1¼ pints/3 cups of the boiling water over the chickpeas. Cover with the lid and simmer until just tender.

5 Towards the end of the cooking time, put the tamarind in a bowl and break up with a fork. Pour over the remaining boiling water and leave to soak for about 15 minutes.

6 Tip the tamarind into a sieve (strainer) and discard the water. Rub the pulp through, discarding any stones (pits) and fibre.

7 Heat the oil in a large pan, add the cumin seeds and fry for 2 minutes, until they splutter. Add the onion, garlic and ginger and fry for 5 minutes. Add the cumin, coriander, turmeric, chilli and salt, and fry for 3–4 minutes. Add the tomatoes, garam masala and tamarind pulp, and bring to the boil.

8 Stir the tamarind mixture into the chickpeas, cover and cook for a further 1 hour. Either serve straight from the cooking pot, or spoon into a warmed serving dish. Garnish with chopped chilli and onion.

Energy 269kcal/1131kJ; Protein 12.6g; Carbohydrate 30.8g, of which sugars 4.1g; Fat 11.5g, of which saturates 1.3g; Cholesterol 0mg; Calcium 98mg; Fibre 6.8g; Sodium 273mg.

GRAM FLOUR PANCAKES <u>WITH</u> FRESH CHILLI CHUTNEY

GRAM FLOUR IS MADE FROM GROUND DRIED CHICKPEAS AND HAS A CREAMY COLOUR AND DISTINCTIVE FLAVOUR. SERVE THESE PANCAKES AND CHILLI CHUTNEY WITH A CHICKEN OR VEGETABLE CURRY.

MAKES ABOUT SIXTEEN PANCAKES

INGREDIENTS
    450g/1lb gram flour
    5ml/1 tsp bicarbonate of soda
    10ml/2 tsp salt
    800ml/28fl oz/3½ cups water
    vegetable oil, for frying
For the fresh chilli chutney
    3 tomatoes, seeded and diced
    60ml/4 tbsp lime juice
    1 red onion, thinly sliced
    2 fresh green chillies, seeded and
      thinly sliced
    45ml/3 tbsp chopped fresh mint

1 To make the pancakes, sift the flour, bicarbonate of soda and salt into a large mixing bowl.

2 Make a well in the centre and pour in the water. Gradually whisk the flour into the water until you have a smooth batter. Leave to stand for 30 minutes.

3 Meanwhile, mix together the ingredients for the fresh chilli chutney and set aside while you cook the pancakes.

4 Pour enough oil into a frying pan to cover the base and heat it over a medium heat. Place 2 tablespoons of the batter into the pan. Fry for about 3 minutes on one side, then, using a metal spatula, turn over and cook the other side until set and golden. Cook several pancakes at once depending on the size of the pan. Drain on kitchen paper and keep warm while you make the remaining pancakes.

5 Serve the pancakes hot, with the fresh chilli chutney.

Energy 108kcal/455kJ; Protein 7.3g; Carbohydrate 12.5g, of which sugars 1.2g; Fat 3.2g, of which saturates 0.4g; Cholesterol 0mg; Calcium 50mg; Fibre 0.2g; Sodium 14mg.

JAMAICAN RICE AND BEANS

THIS TRADITIONAL SIDE DISH IS POPULAR THAN IN JAMAICA WHERE IT HAS BECOME ALMOST A NATIONAL DISH. THE "PEAS" ARE ACTUALLY RED KIDNEY BEANS WHICH GIVE COLOUR AND SUBSTANCE TO THE COCONUT RICE. SERVE AS AN ACCOMPANIMENT TO CHICKEN, FISH, MEAT OR VEGETABLES.

SERVES FOUR TO SIX

INGREDIENTS

150g/5oz dried red kidney beans
500ml/17fl oz/2¼ cups water
1 tsp salt
15ml/1 tbsp vegetable oil
15ml/1 large onion, chopped
3 garlic cloves, chopped
2 fresh red chillies, seeded and chopped
5ml/1 tsp dried thyme
300g/11oz long grain rice
400g/14oz can coconut milk

1 Soak the kidney beans overnight in plenty of cold water. Drain and rinse, then put them into a pan. Cover with fresh cold water and bring to the boil. Allow to boil vigorously for 10 minutes, then reduce the heat, cover the pan, and simmer for 1 hour or until tender.

2 Drain the beans then return them to the pan and cover with 300ml/½ pint/ 1¼ cups of the water and add the salt. Bring to the boil, then reduce the heat and simmer, covered, for 15 minutes.

3 Meanwhile, heat the oil in a large pan and fry the onion for 10 minutes until softened. Add the garlic, chillies and thyme. Fry, stirring, for 1 minute, then add the rice. Stir well until the rice is coated in the onion mixture.

4 Pour in the coconut milk, the remaining water and the beans and their cooking water. Bring up to the boil, then reduce the heat, stir well and cover the pan. Simmer over a low heat for 25–30 minutes until the rice is tender and the liquid has been absorbed. Remove from the heat and allow the rice and beans to stand for 5 minutes in the covered pan.

Energy 295kcal/1240kJ; Protein 10g; Carbohydrate 58.2g, of which sugars 6.7g; Fat 2.7g, of which saturates 0.4g; Cholesterol 0mg; Calcium 66mg; Fibre 4.6g; Sodium 79mg.

JAMAICAN BLACK BEAN POT

MOLASSES IMPARTS A RICH TREACLE-LIKE FLAVOUR TO THE SPICY SAUCE, WHICH INCORPORATES A STUNNING MIX OF BLACK BEANS, VIBRANT RED AND YELLOW PEPPERS AND ORANGE BUTTERNUT SQUASH. THIS DISH IS DELICIOUS SERVED WITH CORNBREAD OR PLAIN RICE.

SERVES FOUR

INGREDIENTS

225g/8oz/1¼ cups dried black beans
1 bay leaf
30ml/2 tbsp vegetable oil
1 large onion, chopped
1 garlic clove, chopped
5ml/1 tsp English mustard powder
15ml/1 tbsp molasses
30ml/2 tbsp soft dark brown sugar
5ml/1 tsp dried thyme
2.5ml/½ tsp dried chilli flakes
5ml/1 tsp vegetable bouillon powder
1 red (bell) pepper, seeded and diced
1 yellow (bell) pepper, seeded
  and diced
675g/1½lb butternut squash or
  pumpkin, seeded and cut into
  1cm/½in dice
salt and ground black pepper
thyme sprigs, to garnish

1 Soak the beans overnight in plenty of water, then drain and rinse well. Place in a large pan, cover with fresh water and add the bay leaf. Bring to the boil, then boil rapidly for 10 minutes. Reduce the heat, cover, and simmer for 30 minutes until tender. Drain, reserving the cooking water. Preheat the oven to 180°C/350°F/Gas 4.

VARIATION
Black-eyed beans, pinto or chickpeas can be used instead of the black beans but they do not look quite so dramatic.

2 Heat the oil in the pan and sauté the onion and garlic for about 5 minutes until softened, stirring occasionally. Add the mustard powder, molasses, sugar, thyme and chilli, and cook for 1 minute, stirring. Stir in the black beans and spoon the mixture into a flameproof casserole.

3 Add enough water to the reserved cooking liquid to make 400ml/ 14fl oz/1⅔ cups, then mix in the bouillon powder and pour into the casserole. Bake for 25 minutes.

4 Add the peppers and squash or pumpkin and mix well. Cover, then bake for 45 minutes until the vegetables are tender. Serve garnished with thyme.

Energy 222kcal/932kJ; Protein 6.9g; Carbohydrate 35.6g, of which sugars 24.8g; Fat 6.7g, of which saturates 1.1g; Cholesterol 0mg; Calcium 139mg; Fibre 7.6g; Sodium 232mg.

VEGETARIAN

Beans are essential in many vegetarian dishes, where they frequently provide the protein and carbohydrate content. These ingredients are the basis for a wide variety of classic dishes from around the world, including Lentil Dhal from India, Moroccan Braised Chickpeas, and Kenyan Mung Bean Stew.

ONE-CRUST BEAN PIE

*THIS FREE-FORM WHOLEMEAL PASTRY PIE ENCASES A RICH TOMATO, AUBERGINE AND KIDNEY BEAN
FILLING. IF YOUR PASTRY CRACKS, JUST PATCH IT UP – IT ADDS TO THE PIE'S RUSTIC CHARACTER.*

SERVES FOUR

INGREDIENTS
  500g/1¼lb aubergines (eggplants)
  1 red (bell) pepper
  30ml/2 tbsp olive oil
  1 large onion, finely chopped
  1 courgette (zucchini), sliced
  2 garlic cloves, crushed
  15ml/1 tbsp fresh oregano or 5ml/
   1 tsp dried, plus extra fresh oregano
   to garnish
  400g/14oz can red kidney beans,
   drained and rinsed
  115g/4oz/1 cup pitted black
   olives, rinsed
  375g/13oz/⅔ cup passata (bottled
   strained tomatoes)
  1 egg, beaten, or a little milk
  30ml/2 tbsp semolina
  salt and ground black pepper
For the pastry
  75g/3oz/⅔ cup plain (all-purpose)
   flour
  75g/3oz/⅔ cup wholemeal (whole-
   wheat) flour
  75g/3oz/6 tbsp vegetable margarine
  50g/2oz/⅔ cup freshly grated
   Parmesan cheese

1 Preheat the oven to 220°C/425°F/
Gas 7. To make the pastry, sift the plain
and wholemeal flours into a large bowl.
Rub in the vegetable margarine until the
mixture resembles fine breadcrumbs,
then stir in the grated Parmesan. Mix in
enough cold water to form a firm dough.

2 Turn out the dough on to a lightly
floured work surface and form into a
smooth ball. Wrap the dough in clear
film (plastic wrap) or a plastic bag and
chill for about 30 minutes.

3 To make the filling, cube the
aubergines and place them in a
colander. Sprinkle the aubergines
with salt, then leave for about 30
minutes. Rinse and pat dry with kitchen
paper. Meanwhile, place the pepper on
a baking tray and roast in the oven for
20 minutes. Put the pepper in a plastic
bag and leave until cool enough to
handle. Peel and seed, then dice the
flesh. Set aside.

4 Heat the oil in a large heavy frying
pan. Fry the onion for 5 minutes until
softened, stirring occasionally. Add the
aubergines and fry for 5 minutes until
tender. Add the courgette, garlic and
oregano, and cook for a further
5 minutes, stirring frequently. Add the
kidney beans and olives, stir, then add
the passata and pepper. Cook until
heated through, and set aside to cool.

5 Roll out the pastry on a lightly floured
board or work surface to form a rough
30cm/12in round. Place on a lightly
oiled baking sheet. Brush with beaten
egg or milk, sprinkle over the semolina,
leaving a 4cm/1½in border, then spoon
over the filling.

6 Gather up the edges of the pastry to
cover the filling partially – it should be
open in the middle. Brush with the
remaining egg or milk and bake for
30–35 minutes until golden. Garnish
with oregano.

Energy 554kcal/2318kJ; Protein 17.7g; Carbohydrate 56.6g, of which sugars 15.7g; Fat 30.2g, of which saturates 4.2g; Cholesterol 13mg; Calcium 295mg; Fibre 11.6g; Sodium 1353mg.

EGG AND LENTIL CURRY

EGGS ARE AN EXCELLENT ADDITION TO VEGETARIAN CURRIES AND, COMBINED WITH LENTILS, MAKE A SUBSTANTIAL AND EXTREMELY TASTY DISH. NUTRITIONALLY, EGGS AND LENTILS ARE AN EXCELLENT SOURCE OF PROTEIN AS WELL AS VITAMINS AND MINERALS.

2 Cook the eggs in boiling water for 10 minutes. Remove from the boiling water and set aside to cool slightly. When cool enough to handle, peel and cut in half lengthways.

3 Heat the oil in a large frying pan and fry the cloves and peppercorns for about 2 minutes. Add the onion, chillies, garlic and ginger, and fry the mixture for a further 5–6 minutes, stirring frequently.

4 Stir in the curry paste and fry for a further 2 minutes, stirring constantly.

5 Add the chopped tomatoes and sugar and stir in 175ml/6fl oz/¾ cup water. Simmer for about 5 minutes until the sauce thickens, stirring occasionally. Add the boiled eggs, drained lentils and garam masala. Cover and simmer for a further 10 minutes, then serve.

SERVES FOUR

INGREDIENTS
  75g/3oz/½ cup green lentils
  750ml/1¼ pints/3 cups vegetable
    stock
  6 eggs
  30ml/2 tbsp oil
  3 cloves
  1.5ml/¼ tsp black peppercorns
  1 onion, finely chopped
  2 green chillies, finely chopped
  2 garlic cloves, crushed
  2.5cm/1in piece of fresh root ginger,
    peeled and chopped
  30ml/2 tbsp curry paste
  400g/14oz can chopped tomatoes
  2.5ml/½ tsp sugar
  2.5ml/½ tsp garam masala

1 Wash the lentils thoroughly under cold running water, checking for small stones. Put the lentils in a large, heavy pan with the vegetable stock. Cover and simmer gently for about 15 minutes or until the lentils are soft. Drain and set aside.

COOK'S TIP
You can substitute red lentils for the green if liked. Red lentils tend to disintegrate more when cooking, which will give a smoother curry.

Energy 585kcal/2441kJ; Protein 14.4g; Carbohydrate 87.3g, of which sugars 5.7g; Fat 15.9g, of which saturates 3.5g; Cholesterol 8mg; Calcium 196mg; Fibre 3.2g; Sodium 131mg.

BULGUR WHEAT, ASPARAGUS AND BROAD BEAN PILAFF

NUTTY-TEXTURED BULGUR WHEAT IS USUALLY SIMPLY SOAKED IN BOILING WATER UNTIL IT IS SOFTENED, BUT IT CAN BE COOKED LIKE RICE TO MAKE A PILAFF. HERE IT IS COMBINED WITH BROAD BEANS, HERBS, AND LEMON AND ORANGE RINDS, WHICH ADD A FRESH, SPRINGTIME FLAVOUR.

SERVES FOUR

INGREDIENTS
  250g/9oz/1½ cups bulgur wheat
  750–900ml/1¼–1½ pints/3–3¾
    cups warm vegetable stock
  225g/8oz asparagus spears
  225g/8oz/2 cups frozen broad (fava)
    beans, thawed
  8 spring onions (scallions), chopped
  15ml/1 tbsp grated lemon rind
  15ml/1 tbsp grated orange rind
  40g/1½oz/3 tbsp butter, cut into
    small pieces
  60ml/4 tbsp chopped fresh flat
    leaf parsley
  30ml/2 tbsp chopped fresh dill, plus
    extra sprigs to garnish
salt and ground black pepper

1 Place the bulgur wheat in a shallow, ovenproof earthenware dish and pour over 600ml/1 pint/2½ cups of the stock. Season with salt and pepper.

VARIATIONS
• Use fresh green beans and either fresh or frozen peas in place of the asparagus and broad beans and, instead of using dill, stir in plenty of chopped fresh mint along with the parsley.
• If you'd like to add a little extra colour to the pilaff, then stir in some finely shredded red (bell) pepper, or some peeled and seeded wedges of tomato.

2 Cut the asparagus spears into 2.5cm/1in lengths, discarding any hard, woody ends from the stems. Add the asparagus pieces to the dish and gently stir these into the bulgur wheat.

3 Cover the dish tightly and place in an unheated oven. Set the oven to 200°C/400°F/Gas 6 and then cook the bulgur wheat and asparagus for 20 minutes.

4 Meanwhile pop the broad beans out of their skins and stir them into the bulgur pilaff, adding a little more stock at the same time. Re-cover the dish and return it to the oven for about 10 minutes.

COOK'S TIP
Leaving the bulgur wheat to stand for 5 minutes after cooking helps to give it a light fluffy texture.

5 Stir in the spring onions, grated lemon and orange rind. Add a little more stock, if necessary. Cover and return to the oven for 5 minutes.

6 Dot the pieces of butter over the top of the pilaff and leave to stand, covered, for 5 minutes.

7 Add the parsley and dill to the pilaff and stir with a fork. Add salt and plenty of black pepper. Serve hot, garnished with sprigs of fresh dill.

Energy 368kcal/1536kJ; Protein 13.4g; Carbohydrate 56.7g, of which sugars 3g; Fat 10.4g, of which saturates 5.4g; Cholesterol 21mg; Calcium 134mg; Fibre 6.2g; Sodium 79mg.

SAVOURY LENTIL LOAF

IDEAL AS AN ALTERNATIVE TO THE TRADITIONAL MEAT ROAST, THIS WHOLESOME LENTIL AND NUT LOAF IS PERFECT FOR SPECIAL OCCASIONS. IT IS GOOD SERVED WITH A SPICY FRESH TOMATO SAUCE.

SERVES FOUR

INGREDIENTS
- 30ml/2 tbsp olive oil, plus extra for greasing
- 1 onion, finely chopped
- 1 leek, finely chopped
- 2 celery sticks, finely chopped
- 225g/8oz/3 cups mushrooms, chopped
- 2 garlic cloves, crushed
- 425g/15oz can lentils, rinsed and drained
- 115g/4oz/1 cup mixed nuts, such as hazelnuts, cashew nuts and almonds, finely chopped
- 50g/2oz/½ cup plain (all-purpose) flour
- 50g/2oz/½ cup grated mature (sharp) Cheddar cheese
- 1 egg, beaten
- 45–60ml/3–4 tbsp chopped fresh mixed herbs
- salt and ground black pepper
- chives and sprigs of fresh flat leaf parsley, to garnish

1 Lightly grease and line with baking parchment the base and sides of a 900g/2lb loaf tin (pan) or terrine.

2 Heat the oil in a large pan, add the onion, leek, celery, mushrooms and garlic, then cook for 10 minutes, until the vegetables have softened. Do not let them brown.

3 Remove from the heat. Stir in the lentils, mixed nuts and flour, cheese, egg and herbs. Season well with salt and black pepper and mix thoroughly.

4 Spoon the mixture into the prepared loaf tin or terrine, pressing it right into the corners. Level the surface with a fork, then cover the tin with a piece of foil. Place the loaf tin inside a large deep-sided baking tray and pour in enough near-boiling water to come just over halfway up the side of the tin.

5 Cover and cook slowly for 1–2 hours, or until the loaf is firm to the touch.

6 Leave to cool in the tin for about 15 minutes, then turn out on to a serving plate. Serve hot or cold, cut into thick slices and garnished with herbs.

Energy 484Kcal/2019kJ; Protein 23.7g; Carbohydrate 34.1g, of which sugars 5.1g; Fat 29g, of which saturates 5.4g; Cholesterol 69mg; Calcium 238mg; Fibre 8.7g; Sodium 128mg.

PARSNIPS AND CHICKPEAS

THIS INDIAN-STYLE VEGETABLE STEW MAKES AN IDEAL MEAL FOR VEGETARIANS. THE CHICKPEAS ADD SUBSTANCE AS WELL AS VALUABLE PROTEIN TO THE DISH. SERVE WITH WARM INDIAN BREADS.

SERVES FOUR

INGREDIENTS

5 garlic cloves, finely chopped
1 small onion, chopped
5cm/2in piece fresh root ginger, chopped
2 green chillies, seeded and finely chopped
75ml/5 tbsp cold water
60ml/4 tbsp groundnut (peanut) oil
5ml/1 tsp cumin seeds
10ml/2 tsp coriander seeds
5ml/1 tsp ground turmeric
2.5ml/½ tsp chilli powder or mild paprika
50g/2oz/½ cup cashew nuts, toasted and ground
225g/8oz tomatoes, peeled and chopped
400g/14oz can chickpeas, drained and rinsed
900g/2lb parsnips, cut into 2cm/¾in chunks
350ml/12fl oz/1½ cups boiling vegetable stock
juice of 1 lime, to taste
salt and ground black pepper
chopped fresh coriander (cilantro), toasted cashew nuts and natural (plain) yogurt, to serve

1 Preheat the oven to 180°C/250°F/Gas 4

2 Reserve 10ml/2 tsp of the garlic, then place the remainder in a food processor or blender with the onion, ginger and half the chilli. Add the water and process to make a smooth paste.

3 Heat the oil in a large frying pan, add the cumin seeds and cook for about 30 seconds. Stir in the coriander seeds, turmeric, chilli powder or paprika and the ground cashew nuts. Add the ginger and chilli paste and cook, stirring frequently, until the paste bubbles and the water begins to evaporate.

4 Add the tomatoes to the pan and cook for 1 minute. Transfer the mixture to a casserole dish.

5 Add the chickpeas and parsnips to the pot and stir to coat in the spicy tomato mixture, then stir in the stock and season with salt and pepper. Cover with the lid and cook in the oven for 1 hour, or until the parsnips are tender.

6 Stir half the lime juice, the reserved garlic and green chilli into the stew. Re-cover and cook for 30 minutes more, then taste and add more lime juice if needed. Spoon on to plates and sprinkle with fresh coriander leaves and toasted cashew nuts. Serve immediately with a generous spoonful of natural yogurt.

Energy 453Kcal/1899kJ; Protein 14.8g; Carbohydrate 50.1g, of which sugars 16.6g; Fat 23g, of which saturates 4.3g; Cholesterol 0mg; Calcium 148mg; Fibre 15.8g; Sodium 394mg.

SPICY-HOT MIXED BEAN CHILLI

INSPIRED BY TRADITIONAL TEXAN COOKING, THIS CHILLI COMBINES TEX-MEX WITH CLASSIC TEXAN CORNBREAD. THE DELICIOUS TOPPING OFFERS THE STARCH COMPONENT OF THE DISH, MAKING IT A FILLING ONE-POT MEAL WITH NO NEED FOR ACCOMPANIMENTS.

SERVES FOUR

INGREDIENTS

115g/4oz/generous ½ cup dried
   red kidney beans
600ml/1 pint/2½ cups of water
115g/4oz/generous ½ cup dried
   black-eyed beans (peas)
1 bay leaf
15ml/1 tbsp vegetable oil
1 large onion, finely chopped
1 garlic clove, crushed
5ml/1 tsp ground cumin
5ml/1 tsp chilli powder
5ml/1 tsp mild paprika
2.5ml/½ tsp dried marjoram
450g/1lb mixed vegetables such
   as potatoes, carrots, aubergines
   (eggplants), parsnips and celery
1 vegetable stock cube
400g/14oz can chopped tomatoes
15ml/1 tbsp tomato purée (paste)
salt and ground black pepper
For the cornbread topping
250g/9oz/2¼ cups fine cornmeal
30ml/2 tbsp wholemeal
   (whole-wheat) flour
7.5ml/1½ tsp baking powder
1 egg, plus 1 egg yolk lightly beaten
300ml/½ pint/1¼ cups milk

1 Preheat the oven to 150°C/300°F/ Gas 2. Put the beans in a bowl and pour over at least twice their volume of cold water. Leave to soak overnight.

2 Drain the beans and rinse well, then place in a pan with the water and the bay leaf. Bring to the boil and boil rapidly for 10 minutes. Turn off the heat, leave to cool for a few minutes. Pour the beans into a large ovenproof dish and put in the oven.

3 Heat the oil in a pan, add the onion and cook for 7–8 minutes. Add the garlic, cumin, chilli powder, paprika and marjoram and cook for 1 minute. Tip into the casserole dish and stir.

4 Prepare the vegetables, peeling or trimming them as necessary, then cut into 2cm/¾in chunks.

5 Add the vegetables to the bean mixture, making sure that those that may discolour, such as potatoes and parsnips, are submerged. It doesn't matter if the other vegetables are not completely covered. Cover with the lid and bake for 3 hours, or until the beans are tender.

6 Add the stock cube and chopped tomatoes to the cooking pot, then stir in the tomato purée and season with salt and ground black pepper. Replace the lid and bake for a further 30 minutes until the mixture is at boiling point.

7 To make the topping, combine the cornmeal, flour, baking powder and a pinch of salt in a bowl. Make a well in the centre and add the egg, egg yolk and milk. Mix, then spoon over the bean mixture. Cover and cook for 1 hour, or until the topping is firm and cooked.

Energy 613Kcal/2595kJ; Protein 29.6g; Carbohydrate 97.4g, of which sugars 15.8g; Fat 14.5g, of which saturates 3.4g; Cholesterol 112mg; Calcium 257mg; Fibre 13.4g; Sodium 413mg.

SWEET-AND-SOUR MIXED BEAN HOTPOT

THIS IMPRESSIVE-LOOKING DISH, TOPPED WITH SLICED POTATOES, IS INCREDIBLY EASY, MAKING THE MOST OF DRIED AND CANNED INGREDIENTS FROM THE KITCHEN CUPBOARD AND COMBINING THEM WITH A DELICIOUSLY RICH AND TANGY TOMATO SAUCE.

SERVES SIX

INGREDIENTS

40g/1½oz/3 tbsp butter
4 shallots, peeled and finely chopped
40g/1½oz/⅓ cup plain (all-purpose)
   or wholemeal (whole-wheat) flour
300ml/½ pint/1¼ cups passata
   (bottled strained tomatoes)
120ml/4fl oz/½ cup unsweetened
   apple juice
60ml/4 tbsp soft light brown sugar
60ml/4 tbsp tomato ketchup
60ml/4 tbsp dry sherry
60ml/4 tbsp cider vinegar
60ml/4 tbsp light soy sauce
400g/14oz can butter (lima) beans
400g/14oz can flageolet (small
   cannellini) beans
400g/14oz can chickpeas
175g/6oz green beans, cut into
   2.5cm/1in lengths
225g/8oz/3 cups mushrooms, sliced
15ml/1 tbsp chopped fresh thyme
15ml/1 tbsp fresh marjoram
450g/1lb unpeeled potatoes
15ml/1 tbsp olive oil
salt and ground black pepper
fresh herbs, to garnish

1 Melt the butter in a pan, add the shallots and fry gently for 5–6 minutes, until softened. Add the flour and cook for 1 minute, stirring all the time, then gradually stir in the passata.

2 Add the apple juice, sugar, tomato ketchup, sherry, vinegar and light soy sauce to the pan and stir in. Bring the mixture to the boil, stirring constantly until it thickens. Season. Preheat the oven to 180°C/350°F/Gas 4.

VARIATIONS
• You can vary the proportions and types of beans used, depending on what you have in the store cupboard (pantry).
• Kidney beans and borlotti beans would work well and can be either interchanged with any of the beans used here, or combined with them.

3 Rinse the beans and chickpeas and drain well. Place them in an ovenproof dish with the green beans and mushrooms and pour over the sauce. Add the thyme and marjoram. Stir well.

4 Thinly slice the potatoes and par-boil them for 5 minutes. Drain well.

5 Arrange the potato slices on top of the beans, overlapping them slightly. Brush with half the olive oil. Cover and cook for 1 hour, or until the potatoes are just tender.

6 Uncover and brush the remaining oil over the potatoes. Cook for a further 30 minutes, to brown the potato topping. Serve garnished with herbs.

Energy 483Kcal/2042kJ; Protein 18.5g; Carbohydrate 73.3g, of which sugars 24.8g; Fat 13.8g, of which saturates 4.5g; Cholesterol 14mg; Calcium 134mg; Fibre 10.9g; Sodium 826mg.

BUTTER BEAN TAGINE

YOU EITHER LOVE OR HATE BUTTER BEANS. THIS HEARTY DISH IS SUBSTANTIAL ENOUGH TO BE SERVED ON ITS OWN OR WITH A LEAFY SALAD AND FRESH, CRUSTY BREAD.

SERVES FOUR

INGREDIENTS

115g/4oz/⅔ cup butter (lima) beans,
  soaked overnight
30–45ml/2–3 tbsp olive oil
1 onion, chopped
2–3 garlic cloves, crushed
25g/1oz fresh root ginger, peeled
  and chopped
pinch of saffron threads
16 cherry tomatoes
generous pinch of sugar
handful of fleshy black olives, pitted
5ml/1 tsp ground cinnamon
5ml/1 tsp paprika
small bunch of flat leaf parsley
salt and ground black pepper

1 Rinse the beans and place them in a large pan with plenty of water. Bring to the boil and boil for about 10 minutes, then reduce the heat and simmer gently for 1–1½ hours until tender. Drain the beans and refresh under cold water.

2 Heat the olive oil in a heavy pan. Add the onion, garlic and ginger, and cook for about 10 minutes, or until softened but not browned. Stir in the saffron threads, followed by the cherry tomatoes and a sprinkling of sugar.

3 As the tomatoes begin to soften, stir in the butter beans. When the tomatoes have heated through, stir in the olives, ground cinnamon and paprika. Season to taste and sprinkle over the parsley. Serve immediately.

COOK'S TIP
If you are in a hurry, you could use 2 x 400g/14oz cans of butter beans for this tagine. Make sure you rinse the beans well before adding to the recipe as canned beans tend to be salty.

Energy 117kcal/487kJ; Protein 3.5g; Carbohydrate 8.5g, of which sugars 2.2g; Fat 7.9g, of which saturates 1.2g; Cholesterol 0mg; Calcium 25mg; Fibre 3.3g; Sodium 635mg.

LENTIL FRITTATA

THICK, VEGETABLE-BASED OMELETTES, OTHERWISE KNOWN AS FRITTATA OR TORTILLA, ARE FAMILIAR DISHES IN MANY MEDITERRANEAN COUNTRIES AND ARE DELICIOUS AND TASTY.

SERVES FOUR TO SIX

INGREDIENTS
    75g/3oz/scant ½ cup green lentils
    225g/8oz small broccoli florets
    2 red onions, halved and thickly
        sliced
    30ml/2 tbsp olive oil
    8 eggs
    45ml/3 tbsp milk or water
    45ml/3 tbsp chopped mixed
        herbs, such as oregano, parsley,
        tarragon and chives, plus extra
        sprigs to garnish
    175g/6oz cherry tomatoes, halved
    salt and ground black pepper

1 Place the lentils in a pan, cover with cold water and bring to the boil, reduce the heat and simmer for 25 minutes until tender. Add the broccoli, return to the boil and cook for 1 minute.

2 Meanwhile, place the onion slices and olive oil in a shallow earthenware dish about 23–25cm/9–10in in diameter and place in an unheated oven. Set the oven to 200°C/400°F/Gas 6 and cook for 25 minutes.

3 In a bowl, whisk together the eggs, milk or water, a pinch of salt and plenty of black pepper. Stir in the herbs. Drain the lentils and broccoli and stir into the onions. Add the cherry tomatoes. Stir gently to combine.

4 Pour the egg mixture evenly over the vegetables. Reduce the oven to 190°C/375°F/Gas 5. Return the dish to the oven and cook for 10 minutes. Remove from the oven and push the mixture into the centre of the dish using a spatula, allowing the raw mixture in the centre to flow to the edges.

5 Return the dish to the oven and cook the frittata for a further 15 minutes, or until it is just set. Garnish with sprigs of fresh herbs and serve warm, cut into thick wedges.

Energy 212kcal/886kJ; Protein 14g; Carbohydrate 13.9g, of which sugars 5.5g; Fat 11.8g, of which saturates 2.7g; Cholesterol 254mg; Calcium 84mg; Fibre 2.8g; Sodium 106mg.

SPLIT PEA OR LENTIL FRITTERS

THESE SPICY FRITTERS COME FROM THE INDIAN SUBCONTINENT. THEY ARE COUSINS OF FALAFEL.
SERVE WITH A WEDGE OF LEMON AND A SPOONFUL OF FRAGRANT MINT CHUTNEY.

SERVES FOUR TO SIX

INGREDIENTS

    250g/9oz/generous 1 cup yellow split
      peas or red lentils, soaked overnight
    3–5 garlic cloves, chopped
    30ml/2 tbsp roughly chopped fresh
      root ginger
    120ml/4fl oz/$\frac{1}{2}$ cup chopped fresh
      coriander (cilantro) leaves
    2.5–5ml/$\frac{1}{2}$–1 tsp ground cumin
    1.5–2.5ml/$\frac{1}{4}$–$\frac{1}{2}$ tsp ground turmeric
    large pinch of cayenne pepper or
      $\frac{1}{2}$–1 fresh green chilli, chopped
    50g/2 oz/$\frac{1}{2}$ cup gram flour
    5ml/1 tsp baking powder
    30ml/2 tbsp couscous
    2 large or 3 small onions, chopped
    vegetable oil, for deep frying
    salt and ground black pepper
    lemon wedges, to serve

1 Drain the split peas or lentils, reserving a little of the soaking water. Put the chopped garlic and ginger in a food processor or blender and process until finely minced (ground). Add the drained peas or lentils, 15–30ml/ 1–2 tbsp of the reserved soaking water and the chopped coriander, and process to form a purée.

2 Add the cumin, turmeric, cayenne or chilli, 2.5ml/$\frac{1}{2}$ tsp salt, 2.5ml/$\frac{1}{2}$ tsp pepper, the gram flour, baking powder and couscous to the mixture and combine. The mixture should form a thick batter. If it seems too thick, add a spoonful of soaking water and if it is too watery, add a little more flour or couscous. Mix in the onions.

3 Heat the oil in a wide, deep frying pan, to a depth of about 5cm/2in, until it is hot enough to brown a cube of bread in 30 seconds. Using two spoons, form the mixture into bitesize balls and slip each one gently into the hot oil. Cook until golden brown on the underside, then turn and cook the second side until golden brown.

4 Remove the fritters from the hot oil with a slotted spoon and drain well on kitchen paper. Transfer the fritters to a baking sheet and keep warm in the oven until all the mixture is cooked. Serve hot or at room temperature with lemon wedges.

Energy 291kcal/1226kJ; Protein 16.5g; Carbohydrate 38.8g, of which sugars 4.6g; Fat 8.6g, of which saturates 1g; Cholesterol 0mg; Calcium 115mg; Fibre 4g; Sodium 33mg.

LENTIL DHAL

THIS SPICY LENTIL DHAL MAKES A SUSTAINING AND COMFORTING MEAL WHEN SERVED WITH RICE OR INDIAN BREADS AND ANY DRY-SPICED DISH, PARTICULARLY A CAULIFLOWER OR POTATO DISH.

SERVES FOUR TO SIX

INGREDIENTS

40g/1½oz/3 tbsp butter or ghee
1 onion, chopped
2 green chillies, seeded and chopped
15ml/1 tbsp chopped fresh
   root ginger
225g/8oz/1 cup yellow or red lentils
900ml/1½ pints/3¾ cups water
45ml/3 tbsp roasted garlic purée
5ml/1 tsp ground cumin
5ml/1 tsp ground coriander
200g/7oz tomatoes, peeled and diced
a little lemon juice
salt and ground black pepper
30–45ml/3–4 tbsp coriander
   (cilantro) sprigs, and fried onion
   and garlic slices, to garnish

For the whole spice mix

30ml/2 tbsp groundnut (peanut) oil
4–5 shallots, sliced
2 garlic cloves, thinly sliced
15g/½oz/1 tbsp butter or ghee
5ml/1 tsp cumin seeds
5ml/1 tsp mustard seeds
3–4 small dried red chillies
8–10 fresh curry leaves

1 Melt the butter or ghee in a large pan and cook the onion, chillies and ginger for 10 minutes, until golden.

2 Stir in the lentils and water. Bring to the boil, reduce the heat and part-cover the pan. Simmer, stirring occasionally, for 50–60 minutes, until soup-like.

3 Stir in the roasted garlic purée, cumin and ground coriander, then season with salt and pepper to taste. Cook for a further 10–15 minutes, uncovered, stirring frequently.

4 Stir in the tomatoes and then adjust the seasoning, adding a little lemon juice to taste.

5 To make the whole spice mix, heat the oil in a small, heavy pan. Add the shallots and fry over a medium heat, stirring occasionally, until crisp and browned. Add the garlic and cook, stirring frequently, until the garlic colours slightly. Use a draining spoon to remove the shallot mixture from the pan and set aside.

6 Melt the butter or ghee in the same pan. Add the cumin and mustard seeds and fry until the mustard seeds pop. Stir in the chillies, curry leaves and shallot mixture, then swirl the mixture into the cooked dhal. Garnish with coriander, onions and garlic, and serve.

Energy 262kcal/1095kJ; Protein 10.3g; Carbohydrate 26.9g, of which sugars 4.6g; Fat 13.3g, of which saturates 6.2g; Cholesterol 23mg; Calcium 36mg; Fibre 3.1g; Sodium 84mg.

CREAMY LEMON PUY LENTILS

TINY, GREEN PUY LENTILS HAVE A GOOD NUTTY FLAVOUR AND, COMBINED WITH LEMON JUICE AND CRÈME FRAÎCHE, MAKE A DELICIOUS, SLIGHTLY TANGY BASE FOR POACHED EGGS.

SERVES FOUR

INGREDIENTS

   250g/9oz/generous 1 cup Puy lentils
   1 bay leaf
   30ml/2 tbsp olive oil
   4 spring onions (scallions), sliced
   2 large garlic cloves, chopped
   15ml/1 tbsp Dijon mustard
   finely grated rind and juice of
     1 large lemon
   4 plum tomatoes, seeded and diced
   4 eggs
   60ml/4 tbsp crème fraîche
   salt and ground black pepper
   30ml/2 tbsp chopped fresh flat leaf
     parsley, to garnish

1 Put the lentils and bay leaf in a pan, cover with cold water, and bring to the boil. Reduce the heat and simmer, partially covered, for 25 minutes or until the lentils are tender. Stir the lentils occasionally and add more water, if necessary. Drain.

2 Heat the oil and fry the spring onions and garlic for 1 minute or until softened.

3 Add the Dijon mustard, lemon rind and juice, and mix well. Stir in the tomatoes and seasoning, then cook gently for 1–2 minutes until the tomatoes are heated through but still retain their shape. Add a little water if the mixture becomes too dry.

4 Meanwhile, poach the eggs in a pan of barely simmering salted water. Add the lentils and crème fraîche to the tomato mixture, remove the bay leaf, and heat through for 1 minute. Top each portion with a poached egg, and sprinkle with parsley.

VARIATION
Green lentils can be used instead of the Puy lentils used in this recipe. The canned variety speed up the cooking time and just need heating through.

Energy 398kcal/1671kJ; Protein 22.4g; Carbohydrate 39g, of which sugars 5.2g; Fat 18.2g, of which saturates 6.6g; Cholesterol 207mg; Calcium 80mg; Fibre 4.2g; Sodium 106mg.

CHICKPEA RISSOLES

THESE CHICKPEA RISSOLES ARE CAPPETIZING AND CAN BE SERVED SOLO WITH DRINKS OR THEY CAN FORM PART OF A MEZE TABLE. RADISHES, ROCKET AND OLIVES ARE TRADITIONAL ACCOMPANIMENTS.

SERVES FOUR

INGREDIENTS
300g/11oz/scant 1½ cups chickpeas, soaked overnight in water to cover
105ml/7 tbsp extra virgin olive oil
2 large onions, chopped
15ml/1 tbsp ground cumin
2 garlic cloves, crushed
3–4 fresh sage leaves, chopped
45ml/3 tbsp chopped flat leaf parsley
1 large (US extra large) egg, lightly beaten
45ml/3 tbsp self-raising (self-rising) flour
50g/2oz/½ cup plain (all-purpose) flour
salt and ground black pepper
radishes, rocket (arugula) and olives, to serve

1 Drain the chickpeas, rinse them under cold water and drain again. Tip them into a large pan, cover with plenty of fresh cold water and bring them to the boil. Skim the froth from the surface of the water with a slotted spoon until the liquid is clear.

2 Cover the pan and cook for 1¼–1½ hours, or until the chickpeas are very soft. Alternatively (and this is the better method) cook them in a pressure cooker under full pressure for 20–25 minutes. Once the chickpeas are soft, set aside a few tablespoons of the liquid from the chickpeas, then strain them, discarding the rest of the liquid. Tip the chickpeas into a food processor, add 30–45ml/2–3 tbsp of the reserved liquid and process to a velvety mash.

3 Heat 45ml/3 tbsp of the olive oil in a large frying pan, add the onions and sauté until they are light golden. Add the cumin and the garlic and stir for a few seconds until their aroma rises. Stir in the chopped sage leaves and the parsley, and set aside.

4 Scrape the chickpea mash into a large bowl and add the egg, the self-raising flour and the fried onion and herb mixture. Add plenty of salt and pepper, and mix well.

5 Take large walnut-size pieces of the mixture and flatten them so that they look like thick, round mini-burgers. Coat the rissoles lightly in the plain flour. Heat the remaining olive oil in a frying pan and fry the rissoles in batches until they are crisp and golden on both sides. Drain on kitchen paper and serve hot with the radishes, rocket and olives.

COOK'S TIP
Wet your hands slightly when shaping the mixture, as this helps to prevent the mixture from sticking to them.

Energy 552kcal/2312kJ; Protein 21.3g; Carbohydrate 63.7g, of which sugars 8.2g; Fat 25.3g, of which saturates 3.6g; Cholesterol 48mg; Calcium 234mg; Fibre 10.8g; Sodium 95mg.

ADUKI BEAN STUFFED MUSHROOMS

FIELD MUSHROOMS HAVE A RICH FLAVOUR THAT GO WELL WITH THIS ADUKI BEAN AND LEMON STUFFING. THE GARLICKY PINE NUT ACCOMPANIMENT HAS A SMOOTH, CREAMY CONSISTENCY.

SERVES FOUR TO SIX

INGREDIENTS

200g/7oz/1 cup dried or 400g/14oz/
  2 cups drained, canned aduki beans
45ml/3 tbsp olive oil, plus extra
  for brushing
1 onion, finely chopped
2 garlic cloves, crushed
30ml/2 tbsp chopped fresh thyme
  or 5ml/1 tsp dried thyme
8 large field (portabello) mushrooms,
  stalks finely chopped
50g/2oz/1 cup fresh wholemeal
  (whole-wheat) breadcrumbs
juice of 1 lemon
185g/6½oz/¾ cup goat's cheese,
  crumbled
salt and ground black pepper
For the pine nut tarator
50g/2oz/½ cup pine nuts toasted
50g/2oz/1 cup cubed white bread
2 garlic cloves, chopped
200ml/7fl oz/1 cup semi-skimmed
  (low-fat) milk
45ml/3 tbsp olive oil
15ml/1 tbsp chopped fresh parsley,
  to garnish (optional)

1 If using dried beans, soak them overnight, then drain and rinse well. Place in a pan, add enough water to cover and bring to the boil. Boil rapidly for 10 minutes, then reduce the heat, cook for 30 minutes until tender, then drain. If using canned beans, rinse, drain well, then set aside.

2 Preheat the oven to 200°C/400°F/ Gas 6. Heat the oil in a large heavy frying pan, add the onion and garlic and sauté for 5 minutes until softened. Add the thyme and the mushroom stalks and cook for a further 3 minutes, stirring occasionally, until tender.

3 Stir in the beans, breadcrumbs and lemon juice, season well, then cook for 2 minutes until heated through. Mash two-thirds of the beans with a fork or potato masher, leaving the remaining beans whole.

4 Brush a baking dish and the base and sides of the mushrooms with oil, then top each one with a spoonful of the bean mixture. Place the mushrooms in the dish, cover with foil and bake for 20 minutes. Remove the foil. Top each mushroom with some goat's cheese and bake for a further 15 minutes, or until the cheese is melted and bubbly and the mushrooms are tender.

5 To make the pine nut tarator, place all the ingredients in a food processor or blender and blend until smooth and creamy. Add more milk if the mixture appears too thick. Sprinkle with parsley, and serve with the stuffed mushrooms.

COOK'S TIP
When cooked, aduki beans have a slightly sweet flavour and mealy texture that blends well with herbs and strongly flavoured ingredients. They are perfect for stuffings, bean pâtés and as a base for vegetable roasts and bakes.

Energy 406kcal/1694kJ; Protein 17.5g; Carbohydrate 25.9g, of which sugars 5.9g; Fat 26.6g, of which saturates 8g; Cholesterol 31mg; Calcium 159mg; Fibre 6.1g; Sodium 573mg.

MOROCCAN BRAISED CHICKPEAS

THIS SWEET AND SPICY VEGETARIAN DISH IS A REAL TREAT. SERVE IT HOT AS A MAIN COURSE WITH RICE OR COUSCOUS OR SERVE COLD AS A SALAD, DRIZZLED WITH OLIVE OIL AND LEMON JUICE.

SERVES FOUR

INGREDIENTS

250g/9oz/1½ cups dried chickpeas, soaked overnight in cold water
30ml/2 tbsp olive oil
2 onions, cut into wedges
10ml/2 tsp ground cumin
1.5ml/¼ tsp ground turmeric
1.5ml/¼ tsp cayenne pepper
15ml/1 tbsp ground coriander
5ml/1 tsp ground cinnamon
300ml/½ pint/1¼ cups vegetable stock
2 carrots, sliced
115g/4oz/½ cup ready-to-eat dried apricots, halved
50g/2oz/scant ½ cup raisins
25g/1oz/¼ cup flaked (sliced) almonds
30ml/2 tbsp chopped fresh coriander (cilantro)
30ml/2 tbsp chopped fresh flat leaf parsley
salt and ground black pepper

1 Place the chickpeas in a pan with plenty of cold water. Bring to the boil and boil rapidly for 10 minutes, then place the chickpeas in a casserole dish, cover with lukewarm water and cover.

2 Place in an unheated oven and set the temperature to 200°C/400°F/Gas 6. Cook for 1 hour, then reduce the oven temperature to 160°C/325°/Gas 3. Cook for another hour, or until the chickpeas are tender.

3 Meanwhile, place the olive oil and onions in a frying pan and cook for about 6 minutes, or until softened. Add the cumin, turmeric, cayenne, coriander and cinnamon and cook for 2–3 minutes. Stir in the stock, carrots, apricots, raisins and almonds and bring to the boil.

4 Drain the chickpeas, add the spicy vegetable mixture and stir. Cover and return to the oven for 30 minutes.

5 Season with salt and pepper, lightly stir in half the fresh coriander and parsley and serve sprinkled with the remainder.

Energy 380kcal/1601kJ; Protein 16.6g; Carbohydrate 52.9g, of which sugars 23.2g; Fat 12.8g, of which saturates 1.4g; Cholesterol 0mg; Calcium 173mg; Fibre 10.4g; Sodium 47mg.

TOFU AND GREEN BEAN CURRY

BEANCURD, ALSO KNOWN AS TOFU, IS AVAILABLE FROM SUPERMARKETS. IT HAS A SILKY APPEARANCE, SOFT TEXTURE AND MILD FLAVOUR THAT BENEFITS FROM BEING COMBINED WITH STRONGER FLAVOURS.

SERVES FOUR TO SIX

INGREDIENTS
  600ml/1 pint/2½ cups coconut milk
  15ml/1 tbsp red curry paste
  45ml/3 tbsp vegetable stock
  10ml/2 tsp palm sugar (jaggery) or
    soft light brown sugar
  225g/8oz button (white) mushrooms
  115g/4oz green beans, trimmed
  175g/6oz tofu, rinsed and cut into
    2cm/¾in cubes
  4 kaffir lime leaves, torn
  2 fresh red chillies, sliced
  fresh coriander (cilantro) sprigs,
    to garnish

1 Pour about one-third of the coconut milk into a wok or large pan. Cook until an oily sheen appears on the surface.

2 Add the red curry paste, stock and sugar to the coconut milk. Mix together thoroughly.

3 Add the button mushrooms. Stir well and cook over a medium heat for about 1 minute. Stir in the rest of the coconut milk and bring back to the boil.

4 Add the green beans and cubes of tofu and allow to simmer gently for another 4–5 minutes.

5 Stir in the kaffir lime leaves and red chillies. Serve garnished with the fresh coriander sprigs.

Energy 63kcal/265kJ; Protein 3.9g; Carbohydrate 8.2g, of which sugars 7.8g; Fat 1.8g, of which saturates 0.4g; Cholesterol 0mg; Calcium 189mg; Fibre 0.8g; Sodium 647mg.

KENYAN MUNG BEAN STEW

THE LOCAL NAME FOR THIS VEGETARIAN STEW IS DENGU. IT IS A GOOD EXAMPLE OF HOW AFRICAN COOKS ADD VARIETY AND NUTRITION TO A DIET THAT DEPENDS LARGELY ON SEASONAL PRODUCE.

SERVES FOUR

INGREDIENTS

225g/8oz/1¼ cups mung beans, soaked overnight
25g/1oz/2 tbsp ghee or butter
2 garlic cloves, crushed
1 red onion, chopped
30ml/2 tbsp tomato purée (paste)
½ green (bell) pepper, seeded and cut into small cubes
½ red (bell) pepper, seeded and cut into small cubes
1 fresh green chilli, seeded and finely chopped
300ml/½ pint/1¼ cups water

1 Put the mung beans in a large pan, cover with water, bring to the boil and boil until the beans are very soft and the water has evaporated. Remove the pan from the heat and mash the beans with a fork or potato masher until smooth. Set aside.

2 Heat the ghee or butter in a separate pan, add the garlic and onion and fry for 4–5 minutes, until golden. Add the tomato purée and cook for a further 2–3 minutes, stirring all the time.

3 Stir in the mashed beans, then add the green and red peppers and chilli.

COOK'S TIP
Mung beans can be found in most Asian shops and larger supermarkets. If unavailable, use whole green lentils.

4 Add the water, stirring well to mix all the ingredients together.

5 Pour the mixture into a clean pan and simmer for about 10 minutes, then spoon into a serving dish and serve immediately.

Energy 229kcal/965kJ; Protein 14.5g; Carbohydrate 31.1g, of which sugars 5.5g; Fat 6g, of which saturates 3.5g; Cholesterol 13mg; Calcium 61mg; Fibre 6.8g; Sodium 65mg.

MUSHROOM AND SUNFLOWER SEED FLAN WITH CHICKPEA PASTRY

THIS FLAN CAN BE PREPARED IN ADVANCE AND IS GOOD WARM OR COLD. THE CHICKPEA FLOUR USED TO MAKE THE PASTRY ADDS A NUTTY TASTE.

SERVES FOUR

INGREDIENTS
   75g/3oz/⅔ cup chickpea flour plus
      75g/3oz/⅔ cup rice flour
   75g/3oz/16 tbsp butter
   45ml/3 tbsp walnut or sunflower oil
   175g/6oz fresh baby corn
   50g/2oz sunflower seeds
   225g/8oz button mushrooms, wiped
   75g/3oz fresh spinach or defrosted
      frozen leaf spinach
   juice of 1 lemon or 30ml/2 tbsp
      cider vinegar
   salt and ground black pepper

1 Heat the oven to 180°C/350°F/Gas 4. Make the pastry by rubbing the butter into the flour.

2 Add enough water to make a firm dough. Roll it out and line a 23–25cm/9–10in flan dish. You can press the pastry out into the flan dish rather than rolling it.

3 Prick the bottom of the pastry case (pie case), line it with foil, and weight it with beans or rice. Bake for 10 minutes with the foil, then 10 minutes without, so that the pastry case becomes crisp.

4 Heat the oil in a pan and add the corn and sunflower seeds. Fry briskly till they are browned all over.

5 Add the mushrooms, reduce the heat slightly and cook for about 3 minutes. Add the chopped spinach, stir well, cover the pan and cook for a few more minutes.

6 Add the lemon juice or vinegar and season well. Make sure the ingredients are well amalgamated, then spoon them into the flan case. Serve the flan at once, or, if you prefer, leave to cool and serve at room temperature.

Energy 447Kcal/1837kJ; Carbohydrate 28.8g, of which sugars 2.5g; Fat 32g, of which saturates 11.7g; Fibre 4.6g; Sodium 401mg.

HARVEST VEGETABLE AND LENTIL CASSEROLE

ROOT VEGETABLES OFFER SOLID, FILLING FARE TO WARM UP THE COLDEST WINTER MONTHS. LENTILS THICKEN THE JUICES AS WELL AS ADDING NUTRITIONAL VALUE TO THIS HEALTHY DISH.

SERVES SIX

INGREDIENTS
  15ml/1 tbsp sunflower oil
  2 leeks, sliced
  1 garlic clove, crushed
  4 celery sticks, chopped
  2 carrots, sliced
  2 parsnips, diced
  1 sweet potato, diced
  225g/8oz swede (rutabaga), diced
  175g/6oz/¾ cup whole brown or
    green lentils
  450g/1lb tomatoes, skinned, seeded
    and chopped
  15ml/1 tbsp chopped fresh thyme
  15ml/1 tbsp chopped fresh marjoram
  900ml/1½ pints/3¾ cups well
    flavoured vegetable stock
  15ml/1 tbsp cornflour
  salt and ground black pepper
  fresh thyme sprigs, to garnish

1 Preheat the oven to 180°C/350°F/ Gas 4. Heat the oil in a large flameproof casserole. Add the leeks, garlic and celery and cook over a low heat for 3 minutes, stirring occasionally.

2 Add the carrots, parsnips, sweet potato, swede, lentils, tomatoes, herbs, stock and seasoning. Stir well. Bring to the boil, stirring occasionally.

3 Cover and bake for about 50 minutes until the vegetables and lentils are cooked and tender, removing the casserole from the oven and stirring the vegetable mixture once or twice during the cooking time.

4 Remove the casserole from the oven. Blend the cornflour with 45ml/3 tbsp water in a small bowl. Stir it into the casserole and heat gently, stirring continuously, until the mixture comes to the boil and thickens, then simmer gently for 2 minutes, stirring.

5 Spoon the casserole on to warmed serving plates or into bowls and serve garnished with thyme sprigs.

Energy 219kcal/928kJ; Protein 10.2g; Carbohydrate 38.7g, of which sugars 12g; Fat 3.6g, of which saturates 0.6g; Cholesterol 0mg; Calcium 98mg; Fibre 8.7g; Sodium 58mg.

INDIAN-STYLE SPICED RED LENTIL AND TOMATO DHAL

THIS IS INDIAN COMFORT FOOD AT ITS BEST — THERE'S NOTHING LIKE A BOWL OF DHAL SPICED WITH MUSTARD SEEDS, CUMIN AND CORIANDER TO CLEAR AWAY THE BLUES. MAKE SURE YOU SERVE IT WITH PLENTY OF BREAD TO MOP UP THE DELICIOUS JUICES.

SERVES FOUR

INGREDIENTS
30ml/2 tbsp sunflower oil
1 green chilli, halved
2 red onions, halved and thinly sliced
10ml/2 tsp finely grated garlic
10ml/2 tsp finely grated fresh root ginger
10ml/2 tsp black mustard seeds
15ml/1 tbsp cumin seeds
10ml/2 tsp crushed coriander seeds
10 curry leaves
250g/9oz/generous 1 cup red lentils
2.5ml/½ tsp turmeric
2 plum tomatoes, roughly chopped
salt
coriander (cilantro) leaves and crispy fried onions, to garnish (optional)
yogurt, poppadums and griddled flatbread or naans, to serve

1 Heat a wok over a medium heat and add the sunflower oil. When hot add the green chilli and onions, stir to combine, lower the heat and cook gently for 10–12 minutes, until softened. Increase the heat slightly and add the garlic, ginger, mustard seeds, cumin seeds, coriander seeds and curry leaves and stir-fry for 2–3 minutes.

2 Rinse the lentils in cold water, drain, then add to the wok with 700ml/1 pint 2fl oz/scant 3 cups cold water.

3 Roughly chop the tomatoes and add them to the wok with the turmeric, and plenty of seasoning.

4 Bring the mixture to the boil, cover, reduce the heat and cook very gently for 25–30 minutes, stirring occasionally.

5 Check the seasoning, then garnish with coriander leaves and crispy fried onion, if liked, and serve with yogurt, poppadums and flatbread or naans.

COOK'S TIP
If you prefer, you can use yellow split peas in place of the lentils. Like red lentils, these do not need to be soaked before cooking.

Energy 302kcal/1274kJ; Protein 16.9g; Carbohydrate 45.6g, of which sugars 8.7g; Fat 7.1g, of which saturates 0.8g; Cholesterol 0mg; Calcium 85mg; Fibre 5.8g; Sodium 47mg.

GARLIC-FLAVOURED LENTILS <u>WITH</u> CARROT <u>AND</u> SAGE

SERVE THESE PUNGENT LENTILS WITH A DOLLOP OF YOGURT SEASONED WITH CRUSHED GARLIC, SALT AND PEPPER, AND LEMON WEDGES.

SERVES FOUR TO SIX

INGREDIENTS
175g/6oz/¾ cup green lentils, rinsed
   and picked over
45–60ml/3–4 tbsp fruity olive oil
1 onion, cut in half lengthways, in
   half again crossways, and sliced
   along the grain
3–4 plump garlic cloves, roughly
   chopped and bruised with the flat
   side of a knife
5ml/1 tsp coriander seeds
a handful of dried sage leaves
5–10ml/1–2 tsp sugar
4 carrots, sliced
5–10ml/1–2 tbsp tomato purée
   (paste)
salt and ground black pepper
1 bunch of fresh sage or flat leaf
   parsley, to garnish

1 Bring a pan of water to the boil and tip in the lentils. Lower the heat, partially cover the pan and simmer for 10 minutes. Drain and rinse well under cold running water.

2 Heat the oil in a heavy pan, stir in the onion, garlic, coriander seeds, sage and sugar and cook until the onion begins to colour. Toss in the carrots and cook for 2–3 minutes.

COOK'S TIP
Cooked in olive oil and almost always served cold this Turkish dish could also include leeks, celeriac, runner or green beans and artichokes.

3 Add the lentils and pour in 250ml/ 8fl oz/1 cup water, making sure the lentils and carrots are covered. Stir in the tomato purée and cover the pan, then cook the lentils and carrots gently for about 20 minutes, until most of the liquid has been absorbed. The lentils and carrots should both be tender, but still have some bite. Season with salt and pepper to taste.

4 Garnish with the fresh sage or flat leaf parsley, and serve hot or at room temperature.

Energy 220kcal/925kJ; Protein 12.7g; Carbohydrate 29.6g, of which sugars 13g; Fat 6.4g, of which saturates 0.9g; Cholesterol 0mg; Calcium 56mg; Fibre 5.8g; Sodium 205mg.

BORLOTTI BEAN STEW

THIS FLAVOURFUL STEW HAS ITS ORIGINS IN TURKISH STREET FOOD. BORLOTTI BEANS ARE THE MAIN INGREDIENT AND HAVE A SWEET TASTE AND A SMOOTH, CREAMY TEXTURE.

SERVES FOUR

INGREDIENTS

175g/6oz/scant 1 cup dried
  borlotti beans, soaked in cold
  water overnight
45–60ml/3–4 tbsp olive oil
2 red onions, cut in half lengthways,
  in half again crossways, and sliced
  along the grain
4 garlic cloves, chopped
400g/14oz can tomatoes
10ml/2 tsp sugar
1 bunch each of fresh flat leaf
  parsley and dill, coarsely chopped
4 ripe plum tomatoes
salt and ground black pepper
1 lemon, cut into quarters

1 Drain the beans, tip them into a pan and fill the pan with plenty of cold water. Bring to the boil and boil for 1 minute, then lower the heat and partially cover the pan. Simmer the beans for about 30 minutes, or until they are tender but not soft or mushy. Drain, rinse well under cold running water and remove any loose skins.

2 Heat the oil in a heavy pan and stir in the onions and garlic. When they begin to soften, add the can of tomatoes, sugar and half the herbs.

3 Add the beans, pour in 300ml/ ½ pint/1¼ cups water and bring to the boil. Lower the heat and partially cover the pan. Simmer for about 20 minutes, until most of the liquid has gone.

4 Meanwhile, bring a small pan of water to the boil, drop in the plum tomatoes for a few seconds, then plunge them into a bowl of cold water. Peel off the skins and coarsely chop the tomatoes.

5 Add the plum tomatoes to the beans with the rest of the herbs – reserving a little for the garnish. Season and cook for another 5–10 minutes. Serve hot or at room temperature, with lemon wedges for squeezing.

Energy 266Kcal/1119kJ; Protein 12.4g; Carbohydrate 34.4g, of which sugars 14.4g; Fat 9.8g, of which saturates 1.5g; Cholesterol 0mg; Calcium 103mg; Fibre 10.6g; Sodium 33mg.

RED BEAN AND MUSHROOM BURGERS

VEGETARIANS AND EVEN MEAT-EATERS CAN ALL ENJOY THESE HEALTHY, LOW-FAT VEGGIE BURGERS.
WITH SALAD, PITTA BREAD AND GREEK-STYLE YOGURT, THEY MAKE A SUBSTANTIAL MEAL.

SERVES FOUR

INGREDIENTS
   15ml/1 tbsp olive oil
   1 small onion, finely chopped
   1 garlic clove, crushed
   5ml/1 tsp ground cumin
   5ml/1 tsp ground coriander
   2.5ml/½ tsp ground turmeric
   115g/4oz/1½ cups finely chopped
      mushrooms
   400g/14oz can red kidney beans
   30ml/2 tbsp chopped fresh coriander
   wholemeal (whole-wheat) flour
      (optional)
   olive oil for brushing
   salt and black pepper
   Greek (US strained plain) yogurt,
      to serve

1 Heat the oil in a wide pan and fry the onion and garlic over a moderate heat, stirring, until softened. Add the spices and cook for a further minute, stirring continuously.

2 Add the mushrooms and cook, stirring, until softened and dry. Remove from the heat.

3 Drain the beans thoroughly and then mash them with a fork. Stir into the pan, with the fresh coriander, mixing thoroughly. Season well.

4 Using floured hands, form the mixture into four flat burger shapes. If the mixture is too sticky to handle, mix in a little flour. Brush with oil and cook in a griddle pan over a high heat for 8–10 minutes, turning once. Serve with a spoonful of yogurt and a crisp salad.

Energy 167kcal/702kJ; Protein 8g; Carbohydrate 20.1g, of which sugars 4.5g; Fat 6.7g, of which saturates 0.9g; Cholesterol 0mg; Calcium 101mg; Fibre 7.6g; Sodium 409mg.

POULTRY
AND MEAT

*Pulses and legumes were traditionally
used to eke out a small quantity of meat or
poultry in a dish, which may have been
expensive or in short supply. Many recipes in
this chapter have become, over the years, long-
standing classic favourites, such as Boston Baked
Beans, French Cassoulet and the
Tex-Mex dish Chilli Con Carne.*

CHICKEN AND SPLIT PEA KORESH

A TRADITIONAL PERSIAN KORESH — A THICK SAUCY STEW SERVED WITH RICE — IS USUALLY MADE WITH LAMB, BUT HERE CHICKEN IS USED TO CREATE A LIGHTER, LOWER-FAT DISH.

SERVES FOUR

INGREDIENTS

  50g/2oz/¼ cup green split peas
  45ml/3 tbsp olive oil
  1 large onion, finely chopped
  450g/1lb boneless chicken thighs
  600ml/1 pint/2½ cups boiling
    chicken stock
  5ml/1 tsp ground turmeric
  2.5ml/½ tsp ground cinnamon
  1.5ml/¼ tsp freshly grated nutmeg
  30ml/2 tbsp dried mint
  2 aubergines (eggplants), diced
  8 ripe tomatoes, diced
  2 garlic cloves, crushed
  salt and ground black pepper
  fresh mint, to garnish
  plain boiled rice, to serve

1 Put the split peas in a large bowl. Pour in cold water to cover and leave to soak for at least 6 hours or overnight.

2 Tip the split peas into a sieve (strainer) and drain well. Place in a large pan, cover with fresh cold water and bring to the boil. Boil rapidly for 10 minutes, then rinse, drain and set aside.

3 Heat 15ml/1 tbsp of the oil in a large flameproof casserole. Add the onion and cook for about 5 minutes. Add the chicken and cook until golden on all sides. Add the split peas, hot chicken stock, turmeric, cinnamon, nutmeg and mint.

4 Bring to the boil, reduce the heat so that the liquid simmers gently, and cover the casserole. Cook for 40 minutes, until the chicken is cooked and the split peas are tender.

5 Meanwhile, heat the remaining 30ml/2 tbsp of oil in a frying pan, add the diced aubergines and cook for about 5 minutes until lightly browned. Add the tomatoes and garlic and cook for a further 2 minutes, stirring.

6 Add the aubergine mixture to the chicken with some seasoning. Mix lightly and cook for 10 minutes, or until the split peas are tender. Sprinkle with fresh mint leaves to garnish and serve with plain boiled rice.

Energy 313kcal/1313kJ; Protein 29.7g; Carbohydrate 21.4g, of which sugars 12.7g; Fat 12.7g, of which saturates 2.4g; Cholesterol 118mg; Calcium 57mg; Fibre 5.7g; Sodium 128mg.

CHICKEN WITH CHICKPEAS AND ALMONDS

THE ALMONDS IN THIS TASTY MOROCCAN-STYLE RECIPE ARE PRE-COOKED, ADDING AN INTERESTING TEXTURE AND FLAVOUR TO THE CHICKEN.

SERVES FOUR

INGREDIENTS
75g/3oz/½ cup blanched almonds
75g/3oz/½ cup chickpeas, soaked
  overnight and drained
4 part-boned chicken breast portions,
  skinned
50g/2oz/4 tbsp butter
2.5ml/½ tsp saffron threads
2 Spanish (Bermuda) onions, sliced
900ml/1½ pints/3¾ cups
  chicken stock
1 small cinnamon stick
60ml/4 tbsp chopped fresh flat leaf
  parsley, plus extra to garnish
lemon juice, to taste
salt and ground black pepper

1 Place the blanched almonds and the chickpeas in a large flameproof casserole of water and bring to the boil. Boil for 10 minutes, then reduce the heat. Simmer for 1–1½ hours until the chickpeas are soft. Drain and set aside.

2 Place the skinned chicken pieces in the casserole, together with the butter, half of the saffron, and salt and plenty of black pepper. Heat gently, stirring, until the butter has melted.

3 Add the onions and stock, bring to the boil, then add the reserved cooked almonds, chickpeas and cinnamon stick. Cover with a tightly fitting lid and cook very gently for 45–60 minutes until the chicken is completely tender.

4 Transfer the chicken and chickpea mixture to a serving plate and keep warm. Bring the sauce to the boil and cook over a high heat until it is well reduced, stirring frequently.

5 Add the chopped parsley and remaining saffron to the casserole and cook for a further 2–3 minutes. Sharpen the sauce with a little lemon juice, then pour the sauce over the chicken and serve, garnished with extra fresh parsley.

Energy 431kcal/1803kJ; Protein 44.4g; Carbohydrate 11g, of which sugars 1.6g; Fat 23.6g, of which saturates 7.9g; Cholesterol 132mg; Calcium 110mg; Fibre 4g; Sodium 180mg.

BURRITOS WITH CHARGRILLED CHICKEN AND FRIJOLES REFRITOS

BURRITOS ARE SOFT WHEAT-FLOUR TORTILLAS USED AS A WRAPPER FOR A RANGE OF FILLINGS. HERE, THEY ARE FILLED WITH STRIPS OF GOLDEN CHICKEN AND THE LATIN AMERICAN SPECIALITY REFRIED BEANS OR FRIJOLES REFRITOS. ALTHOUGH THE NAME IMPLIES THEY ARE FRIED TWICE, THEY ARE ACTUALLY BOILED FIRST THEN FRIED.

SERVES FOUR

INGREDIENTS
  4 skinless chicken breast fillets, cut
    into strips
  5ml/1 tsp paprika
  8 large soft wheat-flour tortillas
  salt and ground black pepper
  Guacamole, grated Cheddar, sour
    cream, shredded iceberg lettuce,
    hot chilli sauce, to serve
For the refried beans
  250g/9oz/1½ cups dried pinto beans
  60ml/4 tbsp olive oil
  1 large onion, chopped
  3 cloves garlic, chopped
  10ml/2 tsp ground cumin
  2.5–5ml/½–1 tsp hot chilli powder
  400g/14oz can chopped tomatoes

3 Heat half the oil in a large frying pan and fry the onion for 10 minutes. Add the garlic, cumin and chilli powder and fry, stirring, for another minute. Add the tomatoes and simmer for 3 minutes.

4 Stir in the beans and cook for about 10 minutes. Season with salt and pepper to taste.

1 Soak the pinto beans overnight in plenty of cold water. Drain and rinse then put them into a pan. Cover with fresh cold water and bring to the boil. Allow to boil vigorously for 10 minutes then reduce the heat, cover the pan, and simmer for 1 hour or until tender.

2 Drain the beans, then put them into a blender or food processor and process until roughly puréed so you have a combination of fully puréed and roughly chopped beans.

5 Meanwhile, mix the paprika with the remaining oil and brush the chicken strips with the mixture then season. Heat a griddle pan until hot and cook the chicken in three batches until golden and cooked through.

6 Warm the tortillas and spoon some of the refried beans over the top, then add the chicken strips and additions of your choice such as guacamole. Roll up the tortillas loosely and serve two per person.

VARIATION
Red kidney beans, borlotti beans or brown beans can be used instead of the pinto beans. You can also mash the beans by hand rather than in a food processor or blender.

MUSHROOM-PICKER'S CHICKEN PAELLA

A GOOD PAELLA IS BASED ON A FEW WELL CHOSEN INGREDIENTS, PARTICULARLY THE RIGHT TYPE OF RICE. HERE, WILD MUSHROOMS COMBINE WITH CHICKEN AND VEGETABLES.

SERVES FOUR

INGREDIENTS
  45ml/3 tbsp olive oil
  1 onion, chopped
  1 small fennel bulb, sliced
  225g/8oz assorted wild and
    cultivated mushrooms
  1 garlic clove, crushed
  3 chicken legs, chopped in half
    through the bone
  350g/12oz/1⅔ cups paella rice
  900ml/1½ pints/3¾ cups boiling
    chicken stock
  1 pinch saffron threads or 1 sachet
    saffron powder
  1 thyme sprig
  400g/14oz can butter (lima)
    beans, drained
  75g/3oz/¾ cup frozen peas

1 Heat the olive oil in a large frying pan or paella pan.

2 Add the onion and fennel, and fry over a gentle heat for 3–4 minutes.

3 Add the mushrooms and garlic, and cook until the juices begin to run, then increase the heat to evaporate the juices. Push the onion and mushrooms to one side. Add the chicken and cook, turning often, until half cooked. If necessary, remove the mushroom mixture and return it to the pan when the chicken is part cooked.

4 Stir in the rice, add the stock, saffron, thyme, butter beans and peas. Bring to a simmer and then cook gently for 15 minutes without stirring.

5 Remove from the heat and cover with baking parchment and a clean dish towel. Allow the paella to finish cooking in its own heat for 5 minutes.

Energy 581kcal/2430kJ; Protein 30.9g; Carbohydrate 87.2g, of which sugars 3.2g; Fat 12g, of which saturates 2g; Cholesterol 79mg; Calcium 59mg; Fibre 7.4g; Sodium 496mg.

BALTI CHICKEN WITH SPLIT PEAS

THIS IS RATHER AN UNUSUAL COMBINATION OF FLAVOURS AND TEXTURES BUT IT WORKS NEVERTHELESS. THE MANGO POWDER GIVES A DELICIOUS TANGY FLAVOUR TO THIS SPICY DISH.

SERVES FOUR TO SIX

INGREDIENTS
   75g/3oz/½ cup yellow split peas
   60ml/4 tbsp corn oil
   2 leeks, chopped
   6 large dried red chillies
   4 curry leaves
   5ml/1 tsp mustard seeds
   10ml/2 tsp mango powder
   2 tomatoes, chopped
   2.5ml/½ tsp chilli powder
   5ml/1 tsp ground coriander
   5ml/1 tsp salt
   450g/1lb/3¼ cups skinless, boneless
     chicken, cubed
   1 tbsp chopped fresh coriander
     (cilantro)

1 Soak the split peas overnight. Drain and wash them. Remove any stones.

2 Put the split peas into a pan with enough water to cover, and boil for about 45 minutes, until they are soft but not mushy. Drain and set to one side in a bowl.

3 Heat the oil in a deep frying pan, balti pan or skillet. Lower the heat slightly and add the leeks, dried red chillies, curry leaves and mustard seeds. Stir-fry gently for a few minutes.

4 Add the mango powder, tomatoes, chilli powder, ground coriander, salt and chicken, and stir-fry for 7–10 minutes.

5 Mix in the cooked split peas and fry for a further 2 minutes, or until you are sure that the chicken is cooked right through.

6 Garnish with fresh coriander.

Energy 196kcal/822kJ; Protein 20.3g; Carbohydrate 9.8g, of which sugars 2.6g; Fat 8.7g, of which saturates 1.2g; Cholesterol 47mg; Calcium 41mg; Fibre 2.5g; Sodium 51mg.

SLOW-COOKER BOSTON BAKED BEANS

THE SLOW COOKER WAS ACTUALLY INVENTED FOR MAKING BAKED BEANS. MOLASSES GIVES THE BEANS A VERY RICH FLAVOUR AND DARK COLOUR, BUT YOU CAN REPLACE IT WITH MAPLE SYRUP IF YOU PREFER.

SERVES EIGHT

INGREDIENTS

450g/1lb/2½ cups dried haricot
    (navy) beans
4 whole cloves
2 onions, peeled
1 bay leaf
90ml/6 tbsp tomato ketchup
30ml/2 tbsp molasses
30ml/2 tbsp dark brown sugar
15ml/1 tbsp Dijon-style mustard
475ml/16fl oz/2 cups unsalted
    vegetable stock
225g/8oz piece of salt pork
salt and ground black pepper

1 Rinse the beans, then place in a large bowl. Cover with cold water and leave to soak for at least 8 hours or overnight.

2 Drain and rinse the beans. Place them in a large pan, cover with plenty of cold water and bring to the boil. Boil gently for about 10 minutes, then drain and tip into the dish for the slow cooker.

3 Stick 2 cloves in each of the onions. Add them to the pot with the bay leaf, burying them in the beans.

4 In a bowl, blend together the ketchup, molasses, sugar, mustard and stock, and pour over the beans. Add more stock, or water, if necessary, so that the beans are almost covered with liquid. Cover with the lid and switch the slow cooker to low. Cook for 2–3 hours.

5 Towards the end of the cooking time, place the salt pork in a pan of boiling water and cook for 3 minutes.

6 Using a sharp knife, score the pork rind in deep 1.5cm/½in cuts. Add the salt pork to the cooking pot, pushing it down just below the surface of the beans, skin side up. Cover the pot with the lid and cook for a further 2–3 hours, until the pork and beans are tender.

7 Remove the pork from the beans and set aside until cool enough to handle, Using a sharp knife, slice off the rind and fat and finely slice the meat.

8 Using a spoon, skim off any fat from the top of the beans, then stir in the pieces of meat. Taste before adding salt and black pepper, and serve hot.

COOK'S TIP
To cook the beans in a conventional oven, place them in a flameproof casserole. Cook at 150°C/300°F/Gas 2 for 1½–2 hours in step 4, until the beans are just tender. In step 6, cook for a further 1½–2 hours, or until both meat and beans are thoroughly cooked.

Energy 235kcal/997kJ; Protein 19.2g; Carbohydrate 37.4g, of which sugars 13g; Fat 2g, of which saturates 0.5g; Cholesterol 18mg; Calcium 92mg; Fibre 9.5g; Sodium 221mg.

PORK WITH CHICKPEAS AND ORANGE

THIS WINTER SPECIALITY IS A FAMILIAR DISH IN CRETE. ALL YOU NEED TO SERVE WITH THIS LOVELY DISH IS FRESH BREAD AND A BOWL OF BLACK OLIVES.

SERVES FOUR

INGREDIENTS
   350g/12oz/1¾ cups dried chickpeas,
     soaked overnight in water to cover
   75–90ml/5–6 tbsp extra virgin
     olive oil
   675g/1½lb boneless leg of pork, cut
     into large cubes
   1 large onion, sliced
   2 garlic cloves, chopped
   400g/14oz can chopped tomatoes
   grated rind of 1 orange
   1 small dried red chilli
   salt and ground black pepper

1 Drain the chickpeas, rinse them under cold water and drain them again. Place them in a large, heavy pan. Pour in enough cold water to cover generously, put a lid on the pan and bring to the boil.

2 Skim the surface, replace the lid and cook gently for 1–1½ hours, depending on the age and pedigree of the chickpeas. Alternatively, cook them in a pressure cooker for 20 minutes under full pressure. When the chickpeas are soft, drain them, reserving the cooking liquid, and set them aside.

3 Heat the olive oil in the clean pan and brown the meat cubes in batches. As each cube browns, lift it out with a slotted spoon and put it on a plate. When all the meat cubes have been browned, add the onion to the oil remaining in the pan and sauté the slices until light golden. Stir in the garlic, then as soon as it becomes aromatic, add the tomatoes and orange rind.

4 Crumble in the chilli. Return the chickpeas and meat to the pan, and pour in enough of the reserved cooking liquid to cover. Add the black pepper, but not salt at this stage.

5 Mix well, cover the pan and simmer for about 1 hour, until the meat is tender. Stir occasionally and add more of the reserved liquid if needed. The result should be a moist casserole; not soupy, but not dry either. Season with salt before serving.

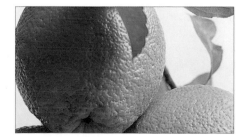

VARIATION
Chickpeas are used in this classic Greek dish but you could also use cannellini or haricot (navy) beans.

Energy 645kcal/2706kJ; Protein 56.1g; Carbohydrate 50.5g, of which sugars 8.2g; Fat 25.6g, of which saturates 4.9g; Cholesterol 106mg; Calcium 171mg; Fibre 11.1g; Sodium 163mg.

PORK TENDERLOIN <u>WITH</u> SPINACH <u>AND</u> PUY LENTILS

LEAN PORK TENDERLOIN IS SUCCULENT AND DELICIOUS WRAPPED IN SPINACH AND COOKED ON A BED OF TINY FRENCH PUY LENTILS, FLAVOURED WITH COCONUT.

SERVES FOUR

INGREDIENTS
  500–675g/1¼–1½lb pork tenderloin
  15ml/1 tbsp sunflower oil
  15g/½oz/1 tbsp butter
  8–12 large spinach leaves
  1 onion, chopped
  1 garlic clove, finely chopped
  2.5cm/1in piece fresh root ginger,
   finely grated
  1 red chilli, finely chopped (optional)
  250g/9oz/generous 1 cup Puy lentils
  750ml/1¼ pints/3 cups chicken or
   vegetable stock
  200ml/7fl oz/scant 1 cup
   coconut cream
  salt and ground black pepper

1 Cut the pork tenderloin widthways into two equal pieces. Season well with salt and ground black pepper.

2 Heat the sunflower oil and butter in a heavy frying pan, add the pork tenderloin and cook over a high heat until browned on all sides. Remove the meat from the pan using a metal spatula and set aside.

3 Meanwhile, add the spinach leaves to a large pan of boiling water and cook for 1 minute, or until just wilted. Drain immediately in a colander and refresh under cold running water. Drain well.

4 Arrange the spinach leaves on the work surface, overlapping them to form a rectangle. Put the pork on top, wrap the leaves around the pork to enclose it.

5 Add the onion to the oil in the frying pan and cook for about 5 minutes, stirring occasionally, until softened. Add the chopped garlic, grated ginger and finely chopped chilli, if using, and fry for a further 1 minute.

6 Add the lentils to the onion mixture in the frying pan and then stir in the chicken or vegetable stock. Bring to the boil, then boil rapidly for 10 minutes.

7 Preheat the oven to 190°C/375°F/ Gas 5. Remove the pan from the heat and stir in the coconut cream until well blended. Transfer the onion and lentil mixture to an ovenproof casserole and arrange the pork tenderloins on top.

8 Cover the casserole and cook in the oven for 45 minutes, or until the lentils and pork are cooked.

9 To serve, remove the spinach-wrapped pork tenderloins from the casserole using a slotted spoon or tongs and cut the pork into thick slices. Stir the lentils and spoon them, with some of the cooking juices, on to warmed, individual plates and top each portion with a few of the pork slices.

VARIATIONS
• Wrap the pork in slices of prosciutto, instead of the spinach leaves, and tie in place with string or secure with wooden cocktail sticks (toothpicks).
• Use 4 large chicken or duck breast portions in place of the pork tenderloin. Check the chicken or duck after about 30 minutes cooking time. Cut the breast portions into thick, diagonal slices to serve. The chicken would also be good wrapped with prosciutto.

Energy 410kcal/1729kJ; Protein 42.7g; Carbohydrate 34.4g, of which sugars 4.3g; Fat 12.3g, of which saturates 4.3g; Cholesterol 87mg; Calcium 93mg; Fibre 6g; Sodium 191mg.

ITALIAN PORK SAUSAGE STEW

THIS HEARTY CASSEROLE, MADE WITH SPICY SAUSAGES AND HARICOT BEANS, IS FLAVOURED WITH FRAGRANT FRESH HERBS AND DRY ITALIAN WINE. SERVE WITH ITALIAN BREAD FOR MOPPING UP THE DELICIOUS JUICES. REMEMBER TO LEAVE TIME FOR THE BEANS TO SOAK BEFORE COOKING.

3 Meanwhile, heat the oil in a pan and cook the sausages until browned all over. Transfer to the casserole and pour away all but 15ml/1 tbsp of the fat.

4 Preheat the oven to 160°C/325°F/ Gas 3. Add the onion and celery to the pan and cook gently for 5 minutes until softened but not coloured. Add the wine, rosemary and bay leaf and bring to the boil. Pour over the sausages, add the stock. Cover and cook in the oven for about 1½ hours.

SERVES FOUR

INGREDIENTS
   225g/8oz/1½ cups dried haricot
      (navy) beans
   2 sprigs fresh thyme
   30ml/2 tsp olive oil
   450g/1lb fresh Italian pork sausages
   1 onion, finely chopped
   2 sticks celery, finely diced
   300ml/½ pint/1¼ cups dry red or
      white wine, preferably Italian
   1 fresh rosemary sprig
   1 bay leaf
   300ml/½ pint/1¼ cups boiling
      vegetable stock
   200g/7oz can chopped tomatoes
   ¼ head dark green cabbage such as
      cavolo nero or Savoy, finely
      shredded
   salt and ground black pepper
   chopped fresh thyme, to garnish
   crusty Italian bread, to serve

1 Put the haricot beans in a large bowl and cover with cold water. Leave to soak for at least 8 hours, or overnight.

2 Drain the beans and place in a pan with the thyme sprigs and at least twice their volume of cold water. Bring to the boil and boil steadily for 10 minutes, then drain and place in a casserole, discarding the thyme.

5 Stir the tomatoes and cabbage into the stew. Season to taste. Cover and cook for about 30 minutes, or until the cabbage is tender. Divide among warmed plates, garnish with chopped fresh thyme and serve with crusty Italian bread.

COOK'S TIP
The stew can be made in a casserole on the hob. The sausages and onions can be browned in the casserole, then the bean mixture simmered gently for about 1¼ hours, or until tender. Softening the cabbage will take about 20 minutes.

Energy 620Kcal/2593kJ; Protein 28.4g; Carbohydrate 47.4g, of which sugars 9.9g; Fat 30.9g, of which saturates 10.8g; Cholesterol 67.5mg; Calcium 205mg; Fibre 7.6g; Sodium 1139mg.

BLACK BEAN STEW

TOLOSA IN THE BASQUE COUNTRY IS FAMOUS FOR ITS BLACK BEAN STEW MADE SPICY WITH VARIOUS SAUSAGES AND PICKLED PORK. HERE IS A SIMPLIFIED VERSION, WITH EXTRA FRESH VEGETABLES THAT ADD WONDERFULLY TO ITS FLAVOUR.

SERVES FIVE TO SIX

INGREDIENTS
275g/10oz/1½ cups black
   beans, soaked overnight
   in cold water
675g/1½lb boneless belly
   pork rashers (strips)
60ml/4 tbsp olive oil
350g/12oz baby (pearl) onions
2 celery sticks, thickly sliced
150g/5oz chorizo, cut into chunks
10ml/2 tsp paprika
600ml/1 pint/2½ cups light chicken
   or vegetable stock
2 green (bell) peppers, seeded
   and cut into large pieces
salt and ground black pepper

1 Drain the beans. Place in a pan and cover with fresh water. Bring to the boil and boil rapidly for 10 minutes. Drain the beans and put in an ovenproof dish.

2 Preheat the oven to 160°C/325°F/ Gas 3. Cut away any rind from the pork, then cut it into large chunks.

3 Heat the oil in a large frying pan and fry the onions and celery for 3 minutes. Add the pork and fry for 10 minutes, or until the pork is browned.

4 Add the chorizo and fry for 2 minutes, then sprinkle in the paprika. Tip the mixture into the beans and mix well to combine thoroughly.

5 Add the stock to the pan and bring to the boil, then pour over the meat and beans. Cover and bake for 1 hour.

6 Stir the green peppers into the stew and return it to the oven for a further 15 minutes. Season and serve hot.

VARIATION
This is the sort of stew to which you can add a variety of winter vegetables, such as chunks of leek, turnip and celeriac.

Energy 595kcal/2479kJ; Protein 32.5g; Carbohydrate 30.1g, of which sugars 5.2g; Fat 39g, of which saturates 11.9g; Cholesterol 102mg; Calcium 58mg; Fibre 5g; Sodium 1636mg.

PANCETTA AND BROAD BEAN RISOTTO

THIS DELICIOUS RISOTTO MAKES A HEALTHY AND FILLING MEAL WHEN SERVED WITH A MIXED GREEN SALAD. USE SMOKED BACON INSTEAD OF PANCETTA, IF YOU LIKE.

SERVES FOUR

INGREDIENTS
225g/8oz frozen baby broad
  (fava) beans
15ml/1 tbsp olive oil
1 onion, chopped
2 garlic cloves, finely chopped
175g/6oz smoked pancetta, diced
350g/12oz/1¾ cups risotto rice
1.2 litres/2 pints/5 cups
  simmering chicken stock
30ml/2 tbsp chopped fresh mixed
  herbs, such as parsley, thyme
  and oregano
salt and ground black pepper
coarsely chopped fresh parsley,
  to garnish
shavings of Parmesan cheese,
  to serve (see Cook's Tip)

1 First, cook the broad beans in a large pan of lightly salted boiling water for about 3 minutes until tender. Drain and set aside.

COOK'S TIP
To make thin Parmesan cheese shavings, take a rectangular block or long wedge of Parmesan and firmly scrape a vegetable peeler down the side of the cheese to make shavings. The swivel-bladed type of peeler is best for this job.

2 Heat the olive oil in a flameproof casserole. Add the chopped onion, chopped garlic and diced pancetta, and cook gently for about 5 minutes, stirring occasionally.

3 Add the rice to the casserole and cook for 1 minute, stirring. Add 300ml/ ½ pint/1¼ cups of the stock and simmer, stirring frequently until it has been absorbed.

4 Continue adding the stock, a ladleful at a time, stirring frequently until the rice is just tender and creamy, and almost all of the liquid has been absorbed. This will take 30–35 minutes. It may not be necessary to add all the stock.

5 Stir the beans, mixed herbs and seasoning into the risotto. Heat gently, then serve garnished with the chopped fresh parsley and sprinkled with shavings of Parmesan cheese.

Energy 511Kcal/2132kJ; Protein 18g; Carbohydrate 77.6g, of which sugars 1.6g; Fat 13.9g, of which saturates 4g; Cholesterol 28mg; Calcium 55mg; Fibre 3.9g; Sodium 556mg.

CASSOULET

THERE ARE MANY REGIONAL VARIATIONS OF THIS CLASSIC FRENCH CASSEROLE OF SAUSAGE, BEANS AND ASSORTED MEATS, EACH WIDELY DIFFERENT FROM THE NEXT ACCORDING TO ITS TOWN OF ORIGIN.

SERVES EIGHT

INGREDIENTS
    225g/8oz/1¼ cups dried haricot
      (navy) beans, soaked for 24 hours
    2 large onions, 1 cut into chunks
      and 1 chopped
    1 large carrot, quartered and cut
      into chunks
    2 cloves
    small handful of parsley stalks
    225g/8oz lean gammon (smoked or
      cured ham), in one piece
    4 duck leg quarters, split into thighs
      and drumsticks
    225g/8oz lean lamb, trimmed and cubed
    2 garlic cloves, finely chopped
    75ml/5 tbsp dry white wine
    175g/6oz cooked Toulouse sausage,
      or garlic sausage, skinned and
      coarsely chopped
    400g/14oz can chopped tomatoes
    salt and ground black pepper
For the topping
    75g/3oz/1½ cups fresh white
      breadcrumbs
    30ml/2 tbsp chopped fresh parsley
    2 garlic cloves, finely chopped

1 Drain and thoroughly rinse the beans, then place them in a large pan and add the chunks of onion, carrot, cloves and parsley stalks. Pour in enough cold water to cover the beans completely and bring to the boil.

2 Boil the beans for 10 minutes, then reduce the heat, cover and simmer for 1½ hours, or until the beans are tender. Skim off any scum that rises to the surface and top up with boiling water as necessary. Drain the cooked beans, reserving the stock; discard the onion, carrot, cloves and parsley stalks.

3 Meanwhile, put the gammon into a pan and cover with cold water. Bring to the boil, reduce the heat and simmer for 10 minutes. Drain and discard the water, leave until cool enough to handle, then cut the meat into chunks. Preheat the oven to 150°C/300°C/Gas 2.

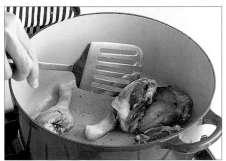

4 Heat a large, flameproof casserole and cook the duck portions in batches until golden brown on all sides. Use a draining spoon to remove the duck portions from the casserole, set aside. Add, and brown, the trimmed and cubed lamb in batches, removing each batch and setting aside.

5 Pour off the excess fat from the casserole, leaving about 30ml/2 tbsp. Cook the onion and garlic in this fat until softened but not coloured. Stir in the wine and remove from the heat.

6 Spoon a layer of beans into the casserole. Add the duck, then the lamb, gammon, sausage, tomatoes and more beans. Season each layer as you add the ingredients. Pour in enough of the reserved stock to cover the ingredients. Cover, and cook in the oven for 2½ hours. Check occasionally to ensure the beans are covered, add more stock if necessary.

7 Mix together the topping ingredients and sprinkle over the cassoulet. Cook, uncovered, for a further 30 minutes.

Energy 378kcal/1586kJ; Protein 31.1g; Carbohydrate 28.5g, of which sugars 6.7g; Fat 16.5g, of which saturates 5.6g; Cholesterol 93mg; Calcium 92mg; Fibre 6.6g; Sodium 581mg.

CLAY-POT LAMB SHANKS WITH BEANS

*A HEARTY WINTER MEAL, THE LAMB SHANKS ARE SLOWLY COOKED IN A CLAY POT UNTIL TENDER ON A
BED OF TASTY BEANS AND VEGETABLES.*

SERVES FOUR

INGREDIENTS

175g/6oz/1 cup dried cannellini
  beans, soaked overnight in
  cold water
150ml/¼ pint/⅔ cup water
45ml/3 tbsp olive oil
4 large lamb shanks, about
  225g/8oz each
1 large onion, chopped
450g/1lb carrots, cut into
  thick chunks
2 celery sticks, cut into thick chunks
450g/1lb tomatoes, quartered
250ml/8fl oz/1 cup vegetable stock
4 fresh rosemary sprigs
2 bay leaves
salt and ground black pepper

1 Soak a clay pot and its lid in a
sink of cold water for 15 minutes. Drain
and rinse the cannellini beans and
place in a large pan of unsalted boiling
water and boil rapidly for 10 minutes,
then drain.

2 Place the 150ml/¼ pint/⅔ cup water
in the drained clay pot and then add
the drained cannellini beans.

3 Heat 30ml/2 tbsp of the olive oil in a
large frying pan, add the lamb shanks
and cook over a high heat, turning the
lamb shanks occasionally until browned
on all sides. Remove the lamb shanks
with a slotted spoon and set aside.

4 Add the remaining oil to the pan,
then add the onion and sauté for
5 minutes, until soft and translucent.

5 Add the carrots and celery to the pan
and cook for 2–3 minutes. Stir in the
quartered tomatoes and vegetable stock
and bring to the boil. Transfer the
vegetable mixture to the clay pot and
season well with pepper, then add the
fresh rosemary and bay leaves and stir
again to combine.

6 Place the lamb shanks on top of the
beans and vegetables. Cover with the
pot lid and place it in an unheated
oven. Set the oven to 220°C/425°F/
Gas 7 and cook for about 30 minutes,
or until the liquid is bubbling.

7 Reduce the oven temperature to
160°C/325°F/Gas 3 and cook for about
1½ hours, or until tender. Season with
salt and serve on warmed plates,
placing each lamb shank on a bed of
beans and vegetables.

COOK'S TIP
An ordinary casserole, which is not pre-
soaked, can be used. When using a
standard ovenproof dish, with boiling
stock added, there is no need to start
cooking at a high temperature; preheat
the oven to 160°C/325°F/Gas 3 instead.

VARIATIONS
• Dried butter (lima) beans or the
smaller haricot (navy) beans can be used
in place of the cannellini beans.
• If you prefer, two 400g/14oz cans
cannellini beans can be used in this dish
– simply place the drained beans in the
casserole with the water and continue
from step 3.
• A variety of other root vegetables would
work well in this recipe – try chopped
swede (rutabaga), sweet potatoes,
butternut squash, parsnips or celeriac
instead of the carrots. In spring, a
mixture of baby turnips and baby carrots
would also be good.

Energy 602kcal/2525kJ; Protein 62.5g; Carbohydrate 33g, of which sugars 13.9g; Fat 25.4g, of which saturates 7.8g; Cholesterol 184mg; Calcium 125mg; Fibre 11.1g; Sodium 178mg.

LAHORE-STYLE LAMB <u>WITH</u> SPLIT PEAS

*NAMED AFTER THE CITY OF LAHORE, THIS HEARTY DISH HAS A WONDERFULLY AROMATIC FLAVOUR
IMPARTED BY THE WINTER SPICES SUCH AS CLOVES, BLACK PEPPERCORNS AND CINNAMON. SERVE WITH
A HOT PUFFY NAAN IN TRUE NORTH INDIAN STYLE.*

SERVES FOUR

INGREDIENTS
  60ml/4 tbsp vegetable oil
  1 bay leaf
  2 cloves
  4 black peppercorns
  1 onion, sliced
  450g/1lb lean lamb, boned
    and cubed
  1.5ml/¼ tsp ground turmeric
  7.5ml/1½ tsp chilli powder
  5ml/1 tsp crushed coriander seeds
  2.5cm/1in piece cinnamon stick
  5ml/1 tsp crushed garlic
  7.5ml/1½ tsp salt
  1.5 litres/2½ pints/6¼ cups water
  50g/2oz/⅓ cup chana dhal or yellow
    split peas
  2 tomatoes, quartered
  2 fresh green chillies, chopped
  15ml/1 tbsp chopped fresh coriander
    (cilantro)

1 Heat the oil in a wok, karahi or large pan. Lower the heat slightly and add the bay leaf, cloves, peppercorns and onion. Fry for about 5 minutes, or until the onion is golden brown.

2 Add the cubed lamb, turmeric, chilli powder, coriander seeds, cinnamon stick, garlic and most of the salt, and stir-fry for about 5 minutes over a medium heat.

3 Pour in 900ml/1½ pints/3¾ cups of the water and cover the pan with a lid or foil, making sure the foil does not come into contact with the food. Simmer for 35–40 minutes or until the lamb is tender.

4 Put the chana dhal or split peas into a large pan with the remaining measured water and a good pinch of salt and boil for 45 minutes, or until the water has almost evaporated and the lentils or peas are soft enough to be mashed. If they are too thick, add up to 150ml/¼ pint/⅔ cup water.

5 When the lamb is tender, remove the lid or foil and stir-fry the mixture using a wooden spoon, until some free oil begins to appear on the sides of the pan.

6 Add the cooked split peas to the lamb and mix together well. Stir in the tomatoes, chillies and chopped fresh coriander and serve.

Energy 331kcal/1379kJ; Protein 26.5g; Carbohydrate 9.7g, of which sugars 1.9g; Fat 20.6g, of which saturates 5.6g; Cholesterol 83mg; Calcium 40mg; Fibre 1.8g; Sodium 99mg.

LAMB AND PUMPKIN COUSCOUS

PUMPKIN IS A VERY POPULAR MOROCCAN INGREDIENT, AND IT TOGETHER WITH THE CHICKPEAS WOULD TRADITIONALLY HAVE HELPED TO MAKE A SMALL QUANTITY OF LAMB GO A LONG WAY.

SERVES FOUR TO SIX

INGREDIENTS
  75g/3oz/½ cup chickpeas, soaked
    overnight and drained
  675g/1½lb lean lamb
  2 large onions, sliced
  pinch of saffron threads
  1.5ml/¼ tsp ground ginger
  2.5ml/½ tsp ground turmeric
  5ml/1 tsp ground black pepper
  1.2 litres/2 pints/5 cups water
  450g/1lb carrots
  675g/1½lb pumpkin
  75g/3oz/⅔ cup raisins
  400g/14oz/2¼ cups couscous
  salt
  sprigs of fresh parsley, to garnish

1 Place the chickpeas in a large pan of boiling water. Boil for 10 minutes, then reduce the heat and cook for 1–1½ hours until tender. Drain and place in cold water. Remove the skins by rubbing with your fingers. Discard the skins and drain.

2 Cut the lamb into bitesize pieces and place in the pan with the sliced onions, and add the saffron, ginger, turmeric, pepper and salt. Pour in the water and stir well, then slowly bring to the boil. Cover the pan and simmer for about 1 hour or until the meat is tender.

3 Peel or scrape the carrots and cut them into large chunks. Cut the pumpkin into 2.5cm/1in cubes, discarding the skin, seeds and pith.

4 Stir the carrots, pumpkin and raisins into the meat mixture with the chickpeas, cover the pan and simmer for 30–35 minutes more, stirring occasionally, until the vegetables and meat are completely tender.

5 Meanwhile, prepare the couscous according to the instructions on the packet, and steam on top of the stew, then fork lightly to fluff up. Spoon the couscous on to a warmed serving plate, add the stew and stir the stew into the couscous. Extra gravy can be served separately. Sprinkle some tiny sprigs of fresh parsley over the top and serve immediately.

Energy 725Kcal/3034kJ; Protein 34.8g; Carbohydrate 115.4g, of which sugars 69.5g; Fat 16.6g, of which saturates 6.8g; Cholesterol 86mg; Calcium 282mg; Fibre 21.5g; Sodium 297mg.

CHILLI CON CARNE

ORIGINALLY MADE WITH FINELY CHOPPED BEEF, CHILLIES AND KIDNEY BEANS BY HUNGRY LABOURERS WORKING ON THE TEXAN RAILROAD, THIS FAMOUS TEX-MEX STEW HAS BECOME AN INTERNATIONAL FAVOURITE. SERVE WITH RICE OR BAKED POTATOES TO COMPLETE THIS HEARTY MEAL.

SERVES EIGHT

INGREDIENTS
    1.2kg/2½lb lean braising steak
    30ml/2 tbsp sunflower oil
    1 large onion, chopped
    2 garlic cloves, finely chopped
    15ml/1 tbsp plain (all-purpose) flour
    300ml/½ pint/1¼ cups red wine
    300ml/½ pint/1¼ cups beef stock
    30ml/2 tbsp tomato purée (paste)
    fresh coriander (cilantro) leaves,
      to garnish
    salt and ground black pepper
For the beans
    30ml/2 tbsp olive oil
    1 onion, chopped
    1 red chilli, seeded and chopped
    2 x 400g/14oz cans red kidney
      beans, drained and rinsed
    400g/14oz can chopped tomatoes
For the topping
    6 tomatoes, peeled and chopped
    1 green chilli, seeded and chopped
    30ml/2 tbsp chopped fresh chives
    30ml/2 tbsp chopped fresh coriander
      (cilantro)
    150ml/¼ pint/⅔ cup sour cream

1 Cut the meat into small cubes. Season the flour and place it on a plate. Toss a batch of meat in it.

2 Meanwhile, heat the oil in a large, flameproof casserole. Add the chopped onion and garlic, and cook until softened but not coloured.

VARIATION
This stew is equally good served with tortillas instead of rice. Wrap the tortillas in foil and warm through in the oven.

3 Use a draining spoon to remove the onion from the pan, then add the floured beef and cook over a high heat until browned on all sides. Remove from the pan and set aside, then flour and brown another batch of meat.

4 When the last batch of meat is browned, return the first batches with the onion to the pan. Stir in the wine, stock and tomato purée. Bring to the boil, reduce the heat and simmer for 45 minutes, or until the beef is tender.

5 Meanwhile, for the beans, heat the olive oil in a frying pan and cook the onion and chilli until softened. Add the kidney beans and tomatoes, and simmer gently for 20–25 minutes, or until thickened and reduced.

6 Mix the tomatoes, chilli, chives and coriander for the topping. Ladle the meat mixture on to warmed plates. Add a layer of bean mixture and tomato topping. Finish with sour cream and garnish with coriander leaves.

Energy 480kcal/2013kJ; Protein 38.6g; Carbohydrate 29.8g, of which sugars 12.4g; Fat 23.6g, of which saturates 8.8g; Cholesterol 114mg; Calcium 127mg; Fibre 9g; Sodium 544mg.

CHOLENT

THIS IS A LONG-SIMMERED DISH OF BEANS, GRAINS, MEAT AND VEGETABLES. THE ADDITION OF WHOLE BOILED EGGS IS A TRADITIONAL FEATURE. START SOAKING THE BEANS THE DAY BEFORE YOU'RE GOING TO USE THEM; THEY NEED AT LEAST 8 HOURS.

SERVES FOUR

INGREDIENTS

250g/9oz/1⅓ cups dried haricot (navy) beans
30ml/2 tbsp olive oil
1 onion, chopped
4 garlic cloves, finely chopped
50g/2oz/1¼ cups pearl barley
15ml/1 tbsp ground paprika
pinch of cayenne pepper
1 celery stick, chopped
400g/14oz can chopped tomatoes
3 carrots, sliced
1 small turnip, diced
2 baking potatoes, peeled and cut into chunks
675g/1½lb mixture of beef brisket, stewing beef and smoked beef, cut into cubes
1 litre/1¾ pints/4 cups boiling beef stock
30ml/2 tbsp easy-cook (converted) white rice
4 eggs, at room temperature
salt and ground black pepper

1 Place the beans in a large bowl. Pour over plenty of cold water to cover and leave to soak for at least 8 hours, or overnight if you like.

2 Drain the beans well, then place them in a large pan, cover with fresh cold water and bring to the boil. Boil them steadily for about 10 minutes, skimming off any froth that rises to the surface, then drain well and set aside.

3 Preheat the oven to 160°C/325°F/ Gas 3. Meanwhile, heat the oil in a pan, add the onion and garlic, and cook gently for about 10 minutes, or until soft. Transfer to a large casserole.

4 Add the beans, barley, paprika, cayenne, celery, tomatoes, carrots, turnip and potatoes to the onion. Mix well and place the meats on top.

5 Cover and cook in the oven for 3 hours, or until the meat and vegetables are very tender. Add the rice, stir, and season with salt and pepper.

6 Rinse the eggs in tepid water, then lower them, one at a time, into the casserole. Cover and cook for a further 45 minutes, or until the rice is cooked. Serve hot, making sure each portion contains a whole egg.

Energy 860Kcal/3607kJ; Protein 58.9g; Carbohydrate 74.2g, of which sugars 13.7g; Fat 38.8g, of which saturates 12.7g; Cholesterol 341mg; Calcium 164mg; Fibre 10.9g; Sodium 639mg.

BEEF AND LENTIL BALLS WITH TOMATO SAUCE

MIXING LENTILS WITH THE MINCED BEEF NOT ONLY BOOSTS THE FIBRE CONTENT OF THESE
MEATBALLS BUT ALSO ADDS TO THE FLAVOUR.

SERVES EIGHT

INGREDIENTS
    15ml/1 tbsp olive oil
    2 onions, finely chopped
    2 celery sticks, finely chopped
    2 large carrots, finely chopped
    400g/14oz lean minced (ground) beef
    200g/7oz/scant 1 cup brown lentils
    400g/14oz can plum tomatoes
    30ml/2 tbsp tomato purée (paste)
    2 bay leaves
    300ml/½ pint/1¼ cups vegetable
      stock
    175ml/6fl oz/¾ cup red wine
    30–45ml/2–3 tbsp Worcestershre
      sauce
    2 eggs
    2 large handfuls of fresh parsley,
      chopped
    sea salt and ground black pepper
    mashed potates, to serve
For the tomato sauce
    4 onions, finely chopped
    2 x 400g/14oz can chopped tomatoes
    60ml/4 tbsp dry red wine
    3 fresh dill sprigs, finely chopped

1 To make the tomato sauce, combine the onions, canned plum tomatoes and red wine in a pan. Bring to the boil, lower the heat, cover the pan and simmer for 30 minutes. Purée the mixture in a blender or food processor, then return it to the clean pan and set it aside.

2 To make the meatballs, heat the oil in a large heavy pan and cook the chopped onions, celery and carrots for 5–10 minutes or until the onions and carrots have softened.

3 Add the minced beef and cook over a high heat, stirring frequently, until the meat is lightly browned.

4 Add the lentils, tomatoes, tomato purée, bay leaves, vegetable stock and wine. Mix well and bring to the boil. Lower the heat and simmer for 20–30 minutes until the liquid has been absorbed. Remove the bay leaves, then stir in the Worcestershire sauce.

5 Remove the pan from the heat and add the eggs and parsley. Season with salt and pepper and mix well, then leave to cool. Meanwhile, preheat the oven to 180°C/350°F/Gas 4.

6 Shape the beef mixture into neat balls, rolling them in your hands. Arrange in an ovenproof dish and bake for 25 minutes. While the meatballs are baking, reheat the tomato sauce. Just before serving, stir in the chopped dill. Pour the tomato sauce over the meatballs and serve. Mashed potatoes make an excellent accompaniment.

Energy 272Kcal/1154kJ; Carbohydrate 22.65g, of which sugars 9g; Fat 9.3g, of which saturates 2.9g; Fibre 4.5g; Sodium 155mg.

FISH AND SHELLFISH

*From Roast Cod with Pancetta and Butter
Beans to Masoor Dhal with Spiced Prawns,
and Red Rice Salad Niçoise, the recipes show
the true versatility of pulses and legumes.
Every eating occasion is catered for, whether
you're looking for a light summer lunch or a
hearty Sunday dinner.*

ROAST COD WITH PANCETTA AND BUTTER BEANS

*THICK COD STEAKS WRAPPED IN PANCETTA AND ROASTED MAKE A SUPERB SUPPER DISH WHEN SERVED
ON A BED OF BUTTER BEANS, WITH SWEET AND JUICY CHERRY TOMATOES ON THE SIDE.*

SERVES FOUR

INGREDIENTS
200g/7oz/1 cup butter (lima) beans,
   soaked overnight in cold water
2 leeks, thinly sliced
2 garlic cloves, chopped
8 fresh sage leaves
90ml/6 tbsp fruity olive oil
8 thin pancetta slices
4 thick cod steaks, skinned
12 cherry tomatoes
salt and ground black pepper

1 Drain the beans, place them in a pan
and cover with cold water. Bring to the
boil and skim off the foam on the
surface. Lower the heat, then stir in the
leeks, garlic, 4 sage leaves and 30ml/
2 tbsp of the olive oil. Simmer for
1–1½ hours until the beans are tender,
adding more water if necessary. Drain,
return to the pan, season, stir in 30ml/
2 tbsp olive oil and keep warm.

2 Preheat the oven to 200°C/400°F/
Gas 6. Wrap two slices of pancetta
around the edge of each cod steak, tying
it on with kitchen string or securing it
with wooden cocktail sticks (toothpicks).
Insert a sage leaf between the pancetta
and the cod. Season.

VARIATION
You can use cannellini beans for this
recipe, and streaky (fatty) bacon instead
of pancetta. It is also good made with
halibut, hake, haddock or salmon.

3 Heat a heavy frying pan, add
15ml/1 tbsp of the remaining oil and
seal the cod steaks two at a time for
1 minute on each side. Transfer them
to an ovenproof dish and roast in the
oven for 5 minutes.

4 Add the tomatoes to the dish and
drizzle over the remaining olive oil.
Roast for 5 minutes more, until the cod
steaks are cooked but still juicy. Serve
them on a bed of butter beans with the
roasted tomatoes.

Energy 449kcal/1883kJ; Protein 44.5g; Carbohydrate 25.3g, of which sugars 3.9g; Fat 19.5g, of which saturates 3g; Cholesterol 84mg; Calcium 85mg; Fibre 9.8g; Sodium 403mg.

MUSSELS IN BLACK BEAN SAUCE

FERMENTED BLACK BEANS ARE SALTED BLACK SOYA BEANS THAT ARE SOAKED IN HOT WATER BEFORE USE. THEY GIVE AN AUTHENTIC CHINESE FLAVOUR TO SEAFOOD, POULTRY, MEAT AND VEGETABLE DISHES.

SERVES FOUR

INGREDIENTS
  2kg/4½lb mussels
  30ml/2 tbsp fermented black beans
  30ml/2 tbsp vegetable oil
  4 garlic cloves, chopped
  2.5cm/1in piece fresh root ginger,
    peeled and finely chopped
  5 spring onions (scallions), sliced,
    green and white parts separated
  60ml/4 tbsp Shoaxing wine or dry
    sherry
  30ml/2 tbsp dark soy sauce
  5ml/1 tsp caster (superfine) sugar
  90ml/6 tbsp water
  5ml/1 tsp cornflour (cornstarch),
    mixed with a little water
  sprigs of fresh coriander (cilantro)

1 Scrub, clean and rinse the mussels well under cold running water. Discard any mussels with broken shells or those that remain open when tapped.

2 Put the black beans into a bowl and cover with just boiled water. Leave to soak for 20 minutes.

3 Drain and partially mash the beans.

4 Heat the oil in a large pan and fry the garlic for a few seconds. Add the ginger and white part of the spring onions and fry, stirring, for a minute until the spring onions have softened.

5 Pour in the Shoaxing wine or sherry, bring to the boil and continue to boil until the liquor has reduced by a third.

6 Stir in the soy sauce, sugar and water. Toss in the mussels, cover, and simmer over a medium heat for 5 minutes, shaking the pan occasionally, until the mussels have opened.

7 Remove the mussels using a slotted spoon and transfer to serving bowls. Discard any that have not opened. Stir the cornflour mixture into the pan with the green part of the spring onions and bring to the boil, stirring. Cook over a low heat until the sauce has thickened slightly. Spoon over the mussels. Garnish with coriander.

Energy 218kcal/921kJ; Protein 27.2g; Carbohydrate 5.1g, of which sugars 2.5g; Fat 8.6g, of which saturates 1.2g; Cholesterol 60mg; Calcium 305mg; Fibre 0.5g; Sodium 852mg.

RED RICE SALAD NIÇOISE

WITH ITS SWEET NUTTINESS, RED RICE GOES WELL IN THIS CLASSIC SALAD. THE TUNA OR SWORDFISH COULD BE BARBECUED OR PAN-FRIED BUT TAKE CARE NOT TO OVERCOOK IT.

SERVES SIX

INGREDIENTS
about 675g/1½lb fresh tuna or
swordfish, sliced into 2cm/¾in
thick steaks
350g/12oz/1¾ cups Camargue
red rice
fish or vegetable stock or water
450g/1lb green beans
450g/1lb broad (fava) beans, shelled
1 Romaine lettuce
450g/1lb cherry tomatoes, halved
unless tiny
30ml/2 tbsp coarsely chopped fresh
coriander (cilantro)
3 hard-boiled eggs
175g/6oz/1½ cups pitted
black olives
olive oil, for brushing
For the marinade
1 red onion, roughly chopped
2 garlic cloves
½ bunch fresh parsley
½ bunch fresh coriander (cilantro)
10ml/2 tsp paprika
45ml/3 tbsp olive oil
45ml/3 tbsp water
30ml/2 tbsp white wine vinegar
15ml/1 tbsp fresh lime or
lemon juice
salt and ground black pepper
For the dressing
30ml/2 tbsp fresh lime or
lemon juice
3ml/1 tsp Dijon mustard
½ garlic clove, crushed (optional)
60ml/4 tbsp olive oil
60ml/4 tbsp sunflower oil

COOK'S TIP
A good salad niçoise is a feast for the eyes as well as the palate. Arrange the ingredients with care, either on a large serving dish or individual salad plates.

1 Make the marinade by mixing all the ingredients in a food processor and processing them for 30–40 seconds until the vegetables and herbs are finely chopped.

2 Prick the tuna or swordfish steaks all over with a fork, arrange them in a shallow dish and pour on the marinade, turning the fish to coat each piece. Cover with clear film (plastic wrap) and leave in a cool place for 2–4 hours.

3 Cook the rice in stock or water, following the instructions on the packet, then drain, tip into a bowl and set aside.

4 Make the dressing. Mix the citrus juice, mustard and garlic (if using) in a bowl. Whisk in the oils, then add salt and freshly ground black pepper to taste. Stir 60ml/4 tbsp of the dressing into the rice, then spoon the rice into the centre of a large serving dish.

5 Cook the green beans and broad beans in boiling salted water until tender. Drain, refresh under cold water and drain again. Remove the outer shell from the broad beans and add them to the rice.

6 Discard the outer leaves from the lettuce and tear the inner leaves into pieces. Add to the salad with the tomatoes and coriander. Shell the hard-boiled eggs and cut them into sixths. Preheat the grill (broiler).

7 Arrange the tuna or swordfish steaks on a grill pan. Brush with the marinade and a little extra olive oil. Grill (broil) for 3–4 minutes on each side, until the fish is tender and flakes easily when tested with the tip of a sharp knife. Brush with marinade and more olive oil when turning the fish over.

8 Allow the fish to cool a little, then break the steaks into large pieces. Toss into the salad with the olives and the remaining dressing. Decorate with the eggs and serve.

Energy 685kcal/2874kJ; Protein 41.8g; Carbohydrate 61g, of which sugars 6g; Fat 32.2g, of which saturates 5.7g; Cholesterol 127mg; Calcium 134mg; Fibre 9.2g; Sodium 760mg.

HADDOCK <u>WITH</u> SPICY PUY LENTILS

DARK BROWN-GREY PUY LENTILS HAVE A DELICATE TASTE AND TEXTURE AND HOLD THEIR SHAPE DURING COOKING. RED CHILLI PEPPER AND GROUND CUMIN ADD A HINT OF HEAT AND SPICE.

2 Meanwhile, preheat the oven to 180°C/350°F/Gas 4. Heat the oil in a frying pan, add the onion and cook gently for 8 minutes. Stir in the celery, chilli and cumin, and cook for a further 5 minutes, or until soft but not coloured.

3 Turn the lentils and the remaining liquid into an ovenproof dish and stir in the onion mixture, Rinse the haddock pieces and pat dry on kitchen paper. Sprinkle them with the lemon juice and place on top of the lentils.

4 In a clean bowl, beat together the butter, lemon rind, salt and a generous amount of ground black pepper. Dot the lemon butter over the fish. Cover and cook for about 30 minutes, or until the fish flakes easily, the lentils are tender and most of the stock has been absorbed. Serve immediately, garnished with the lemon wedges.

COOK'S TIP
Any firm white fish can be cooked in this way. Both cod and swordfish give particularly good results.

SERVES FOUR

INGREDIENTS
    175g/6oz/¾ cup Puy lentils
    600ml/1 pint/2½ cups vegetable
      stock
    30ml/2 tbsp olive oil
    1 onion, finely chopped
    2 celery sticks, finely chopped
    1 red chilli, halved, seeded and
      finely chopped
    2.5ml/½ tsp ground cumin
    4 x 150g/5oz pieces thick haddock
      fillet or steak
    10ml/2 tsp lemon juice
    25g/1oz/2 tbsp butter, softened
    5ml/1 tsp finely grated lemon rind
    salt and ground black pepper
    lemon wedges, to garnish

1 Put the lentils in a sieve (strainer) and rinse under cold running water. Drain well and place in a pan. Add the stock, bring to the boil and reduce the heat. Simmer for 30 minutes, until the lentils are almost cooked.

Energy 354kcal/1492kJ; Protein 39.4g; Carbohydrate 22.7g, of which sugars 1.6g; Fat 12.4g, of which saturates 4.3g; Cholesterol 67mg; Calcium 63mg; Fibre 4.3g; Sodium 153mg.

MASOOR DHAL <u>WITH</u> SPICED PRAWNS

SPLIT RED LENTILS GIVE THIS RICHLY SPICED DHAL A VIBRANT COLOUR AND SOOTHING TEXTURE.
TOPPED WITH SPICED PRAWNS, YOU COULD SERVE THIS DISH WITH THE GRAM FLOUR PANCAKES.

SERVES FOUR

INGREDIENTS

30ml/2 tbsp vegetable oil
1 large onion, finely chopped
3 cloves garlic, chopped
2.5cm/1in piece fresh ginger, peeled
    and finely chopped
10ml/2 tsp cumin seeds
10ml/2 tsp ground coriander
5ml/1 tsp hot chilli powder
5ml/1 tsp turmeric
7 curry leaves
1 carrot, chopped
6 fine green beans, cut into thirds
150g/5oz/1¾ cups split red lentils,
    rinsed
850ml/1½/3½ cups pints
    vegetable stock
salt and ground black pepper
For the prawns
5ml/1 tsp ground cumin
5ml/1 tsp ground coriander
5ml/1 tsp hot chilli powder
30ml/2 tbsp groundnut (peanut) oil
20 raw tiger prawns (shrimp), peeled
    and tail left on, sliced down the
    back and deveined
chopped fresh coriander (cilantro),
    to garnish

1 First prepare the prawns. Mix together the ground cumin, ground coriander, chilli powder and oil in a bowl. Pat dry the prawns using kitchen paper and add to the spices, season with salt, and stir well until the prawns are coated in the spice mixture. Set aside to marinate while you cook the dhal.

2 Heat the oil in a large heavy pan and fry the onion for 8 minutes until softened and beginning to turn golden. Add the garlic, ginger and spices and cook for 1 minute.

3 Next, stir in the curry leaves, carrot, beans and lentils. Cook for 1 minute until coated in the spice mixture then pour in the stock. Bring to the boil then reduce the heat and simmer, half-covered, for 20–25 minutes, stirring occasionally, until the lentils are very tender. Season to taste.

COOK'S TIP
Split red lentils become soft and pulp when cooked, adding a smooth texture to dishes.

4 Heat a large wok. Add the prawns and their spices and stir-fry for a few minutes until they are pink and just cooked.

5 Divide the dhal among four bowls, top with the prawns and garnish with the coriander.

Energy 298kcal/1250kJ; Protein 19.3g; Carbohydrate 28.6g, of which sugars 5.4g; Fat 12.7g, of which saturates 1.5g; Cholesterol 98mg; Calcium 120mg; Fibre 4.7g; Sodium 143mg.

KARAHI PRAWNS AND BLACK-EYED BEANS

THIS SUBSTANTIAL DRY CURRY CONTAINS A PROTEIN-RICH MIX OF BLACK-EYED BEANS, PRAWNS AND PANEER. BLACK-EYED BEANS ARE SO NAMED BECAUSE OF THE SMALL BLACK DOT ON THE SIDE OF THE BEANS. THEY ARE A FILLING ADDITION TO A DISH.

SERVES FOUR TO SIX

INGREDIENTS
  60ml/4 tbsp corn oil
  2 medium onions, sliced
  2 medium tomatoes, sliced
  7.5ml/1½ tsp garlic pulp
  5ml/1 tsp chilli powder
  5ml/1 tsp ginger pulp
  5ml/1 tsp ground cumin
  5ml/1 tsp ground coriander
  5ml/1 tsp salt
  150g/5oz paneer, cubed
  5ml/1 tsp ground fenugreek
  1 bunch fresh fenugreek leaves
  115g/4oz cooked prawns (shrimp)
  2 fresh red chillies, sliced
  30ml/2 tbsp chopped fresh coriander
    (cilantro)
  50g/2oz/⅓ cup canned black-eyed
    beans (peas), drained
  15ml/1 tbsp lemon juice

1 Heat the oil in a deep frying pan or skillet. Lower the heat slightly and add the onions and tomatoes. Fry for about 3 minutes.

VARIATION
Substitute canned chickpeas for the black-eyed beans in this recipe.

2 Add the garlic, chilli powder, ginger, ground cumin, ground coriander, salt, paneer and the ground and fresh fenugreek. Lower the heat and stir-fry for about 2 minutes.

3 Add the prawns, red chillies, fresh coriander and the black-eyed beans and mix well. Cook for a further 3–5 minutes, stirring occasionally, or until the prawns are heated through.

4 Finally, sprinkle on the lemon juice and serve.

COOK'S TIPS
• When preparing fresh fenugreek, use the leaves whole, but discard the stalks which would add a bitter flavour to the dish.
• Paneer is an Indian semi-soft cheese that can be found in some supermarkets and Indian grocers.

Energy 151kcal/629kJ; Protein 8.5g; Carbohydrate 10.1g, of which sugars 6.6g; Fat 8.7g, of which saturates 1.7g; Cholesterol 41mg; Calcium 72mg; Fibre 1.8g; Sodium 445mg.

SALMON TERIYAKI <u>WITH</u> BEANSPROUTS

THIS CRISP BEANSPROUT SALAD IS THE PERFECT PARTNER TO THE JAPANESE DISH, SALMON TERIYAKI. THE TERIYAKI SAUCE GIVES A SWEET AND GLOSSY GLAZE TO THE FISH. TOGETHER THE RECIPES MAKE A VERY HEALTHY MEAL.

<u>SERVES FOUR</u>

INGREDIENTS
 4 small salmon fillets with skin on,
  each weighing about 150g/5oz
 50g/2oz/1 cup beansprouts, washed
 50g/2oz mangetouts (snow peas)
 20g/¾oz carrot, cut into thin strips
 salt
For the teriyaki sauce
 45ml/3 tbsp shoyu (Japanese soy sauce)
 45ml/3 tbsp sake
 45ml/3 tbsp mirin or sweet sherry
 15ml/1 tbsp plus 10ml/2 tsp caster
  (superfine) sugar

1 Make the teriyaki sauce. Mix the shoyu, sake, mirin and 15ml/1 tbsp caster sugar in a pan. Heat, stirring, to dissolve the sugar. Cool for 1 hour.

2 Place the salmon fillets, skin-side down, in a shallow glass or china dish. Pour over the teriyaki sauce. Leave to marinate for 30 minutes.

3 Meanwhile, bring a pan of lightly salted water to the boil. Add the beansprouts, then after 1 minute, the mangetouts. Leave for 1 minute then add the thin carrot strips. Remove the pan from the heat after 1 minute, then drain the vegetables and keep warm.

4 Preheat the grill (broiler) to medium. Take the salmon fillet out of the sauce and pat dry with kitchen paper. Reserve the sauce. Lightly oil a grilling (broiling) tray. Grill (broil) the salmon for about 6 minutes, turning once, until golden.

5 Meanwhile, pour the remaining teriyaki sauce into a small pan, add the remaining sugar and heat until dissolved. Brush the salmon with the sauce.

6 Continue to grill the salmon until the surface of the fish bubbles. Turn over and repeat on the other side.

7 Heap the vegetables on to serving plates. Place the salmon on top and spoon over the rest of the sauce.

COOK'S TIP
To save time, you could use ready-made teriyaki sauce for the marinade. This useful ingredient comes in bottles and is handy for marinating chicken before cooking it on a barbecue. Add a splash of sake, if you have some.

Energy 321kcal/1337kJ; Protein 31.6g; Carbohydrate 5.3g, of which sugars 4.8g; Fat 16.6g, of which saturates 2.9g; Cholesterol 75mg; Calcium 46mg; Fibre 0.6g; Sodium 873mg.

MACKEREL WITH SHIITAKE MUSHROOMS AND BLACK BEANS

EARTHY SHIITAKE MUSHROOMS, ZESTY GINGER AND PUNGENT SALTED BLACK BEANS ARE THE PERFECT PARTNERS FOR ROBUSTLY FLAVOURED MACKEREL FILLETS. SERVE WITH BASMATI RICE.

SERVES FOUR

INGREDIENTS

   8 x 115g/4oz mackerel fillets
   20 dried shiitake mushrooms
   15ml/1 tbsp finely julienned fresh
      root ginger
   3 star anise
   45ml/3 tbsp dark soy sauce
   15ml/1 tbsp Chinese rice wine
   15ml/1 tbsp salted black beans
   6 spring onions (scallions),
      finely shredded
   30ml/2 tbsp sunflower oil
   5ml/1 tsp sesame oil
   4 garlic cloves, very thinly sliced
   sliced cucumber, to serve

1 Divide the mackerel fillets between two lightly oiled heatproof plates, with the skin-side up. Using a small, sharp knife, make 3–4 diagonal slits in each one, then set aside.

2 Place the shiitake mushrooms in a bowl and cover with boiling water. Leave to soak for 20–25 minutes. Drain, reserving the liquid, discard the stems and slice the caps thinly.

3 Place a trivet or a steamer rack in a large wok and pour in 5cm/2in of the mushroom liquid (top up with water if necessary). Add half the ginger and the star anise.

4 Push the remaining ginger strips into the slits in the fish and scatter over the sliced mushrooms. Bring the liquid in the wok to a boil and lower one of the prepared plates on to the trivet. Cover, reduce the heat and steam for 10–12 minutes, or until cooked through. Remove from the wok and repeat with the second plate of fish, replenishing the liquid in the wok if necessary.

5 Transfer the steamed fish to a large serving platter. Ladle 105ml/7 tbsp of the steaming liquid into a clean wok with the soy sauce, wine and black beans, place over a gentle heat and bring to a simmer. Spoon over the fish and sprinkle over the spring onions.

6 Wipe out the wok and place it over a medium heat. Add the oils and garlic and stir-fry for a few minutes until lightly golden. Pour over the fish and serve immediately with sliced cucumber and steamed basmati rice.

Energy 693kcal/2872kJ; Protein 45.5g; Carbohydrate 1.9g, of which sugars 0.5g; Fat 55.9g, of which saturates 10.4g; Cholesterol 128mg; Calcium 35mg; Fibre 0.6g; Sodium 152mg.

INDEX

aduki beans 10, 16, 17
  aduki bean stuffed mushrooms 82
asparagus, bulgur wheat and broad
    bean pilaff 70

bean ribollita 43
beans 6, 10–15 *see also aduki; black;*
    black-eyed; borlotti; broad, brown;
    butter; cannellini; flageolet; haricot;
    kidney; mung; pinto
  bean and hock soup 47
  bean ribollita 43
  black-eyed bean soup 46
  borlotti bean stew 90
  braised bean and lentil soup 42
  red bean and mushroom burgers 91
  sweet-and-sour mixed bean hotpot 75
beansprouts 6, 16, 17
  beansprout and daikon salad 58
  buying and storing 16
beef
  and lentil balls with tomato sauce 114
  chilli con carne 112
  cholent 113
black beans 10
  black bean salsa 32
  black bean sauce 20
  black bean stew 105
  Jamaican black bean pot 65
  mackerel with shiitake mushrooms and
      black beans 126
  mussels in black bean sauce 119
black-eyed beans 10–11
  bean fritters 31
  black-eyed bean soup 46
  peppery bean salad 55
  spicy-hot mixed bean chilli 74
borlotti beans 10, 11
  bean ribollita 43
  bean stew 90
broad beans 6, 11
  broad bean dip with paprika 26
  bulgur wheat, asparagus and broad bean
      pilaff 70
  pancetta and broad bean risotto 106
black-eyed bean soup 46
brown bean salad 54
brown lentils 8, 9
  lentil and pasta soup 39

butter beans 11
  butter bean tagine 76
  roast cod with pancetta and butter
      beans 118

canned beans 14
cannellini beans 11
  bean salad with tuna and red onion 53
  cannellini bean bruschetta 24
  cannellini bean dip 28
  cannellini bean puree 10
  cannellini bean soup 40
  lamb shanks with beans 108
  white bean salad with red pepper
      dressing 52
cassoulet 107
chicken
  Balti chicken with split peas 99
  chicken and split pea koresh 94
  chicken with chickpeas and almonds 95
  mushroom picker's chicken paella 98
chickpeas 6, 12
  chicken with chickpeas and almonds 95
  chickpea rissoles 81
  chickpea soup 41
  chickpea sprouts 16, 17
  falafel 30
  hummus 27
  Moroccan braised chickpeas 83
  parsnips and chickpeas 73
  pasta and chickpea soup 48
  peppery bean salad 53
  spicy tamarind chickpeas 62
chilli
  chilli con carne 112
  gram flour pancakes with fresh chilli
      chutney 63
  spicy-hot mixed bean chilli 74
cooking
  kidney beans 13
  lentils 9
  pulses 14, 15
corn 13
  spicy-hot mixed bean chilli 74
courgettes and tofu with tomato sauce 61
cucumber and tofu salad 54

deep-fried tofu 34

eggs
  creamy lemon Puy lentils 80
  egg and lentil curry 69
  lentil frittata 77
  Spanish-style bean omelette 25

falafel 30
fish
  bean salad with tuna and red onion 53
  haddock with spicy Puy lentils 122
  mackerel with shiitake mushrooms and
      black beans 126
  roast cod with pancetta and butter
      beans 118
  salmon teriyaki with beansprouts 125
flageolet beans 12
  white bean salad with red pepper
      dressing 52
flatulence 11, 13
flour 20
food poisoning 12, 13

garlic
  garlic-flavoured lentils with carrot and
      sago 89
gram flour pancakes with fresh chilli
      chutney 63
green lentils 8, 9
  egg and lentil curry 69
  lentil frittata 77

haricot beans 12
  bean salad with tuna and red onion 53
  bean and hock soup 47
  bean ribollita 43
  cassoulet 106
  cholent 113
  mixed bean soup 38
  slow-cooker Boston baked beans 100
health benefits 6
  beans 15
  legumes 9
  soya 21
herbs 108
hummus 27

Indian-style spiced red lentil and
      tomato dhal 88

mung bean soufflé pancakes 35
mushrooms
    aduki bean stuffed mushrooms 82
    mackerel with shiitake mushrooms and
        black beans 126
    mushroom and bean pâté 29
    mushroom and sunflower seed flan with
        chickpea pastry 86
    mushroom picker's chicken paella 98

nuts
    chicken with chickpeas and almonds 95

onions 53, 59
one-crust bean pie 68

kidney beans 6, 12, 13
    chilli con carne 112
    mushroom and bean pâté 29
    one-crust bean pie 68
    peppery bean salad 55
    spicy-hot mixed bean chilli 74

lamb
    Lahore-style lamb with split peas 110
    lamb shanks with beans 108
    meat, bean and lentil soup 44
leeks 45
legumes 6, 8–9
lemon Puy lentils 80
harvest vegetable and lentil casserole 87
aduki bean stuffed mushrooms 82
lentils 6, 8–9 see also brown; green; Puy;
        red; yellow
    beef and lentil balls with tomato sauce 114
    braised bean and wheat soup 42
    buying and storing 9
    garlic-flavoured lentils with carrot and
        sage 89
    harvest vegetable and lentil casserole 87
    Indian-style spiced red lentil and
        tomato dhal 88
    lentil and pasta soup 39
    lentil dhal 79
    lentil salad with red onions and garlic 59
    lentil soup 37
    lentils with bacon 64
    savoury lentil loaf 72
    sprouting lentils 16, 17
lima beans 6, 11

miso 20
mixed bean soup 38
mung beans 6, 16
    Kenyan mung bean stew 85

pancetta and broad bean risotto 106
pancetta and butter beans with roast cod 118
parsnips and chickpeas 73
pasta and chickpea soup 48
peanuts 9
    spicy peanut soup 45
peas 6, 8–9
    buying and storing 9
    chicken and split pea koresh 94
    karahi prawns and black-eyed beans 124
    split pea and shallot mash 60
    split pea or lentil fritters 78
peppers 50
    peppery bean salad 55
pigeon peas 6, 15
pine nuts 82
pinto beans 12
    pinto bean salsa 33
pork
    bean and hock soup 47
    black bean stew 105
    cassoulet 106
    Italian pork sausage stew 104
    pork tenderloin with spinach and
        Puy lentils 102
    pork with chickpeas and orange 101
    slow-cooker Boston baked beans 100
pulses 6, 10–15
Puy lentils 9
    creamy lemon Puy lentils 80
    haddock with spicy Puy lentils 122
    pork tenderloin with spinach and
        Puy lentils 102
    puy lentil and cabbage salad 57

red bean and mushroom burgers 91
red lentils 6, 8, 9
    masoor dhal with spiced prawns 123

split pea or lentil fritters 78

shallot and split pea mash 60
shellfish
    karahi prawns and black-eyed beans 124
    masoor dhal with spiced prawns 123
    mussels in black bean sauce 119
soya beans 6, 13
    products 18–21
    sauces 20
spinach and Puy lentils with pork
    tenderloin 102

tofu 18
    courgettes and tofu with tomato sauce 61
    tofu and cucumber salad 54
    tofu and green bean curry 84
tomatoes
    butter bean tagine 76
    courgettes and tofu with tomato sauce 61

urd beans 6, 15

vegetables
    harvest vegetable and lentil casserole 87

yellow lentils 8, 9
    Balti chicken with lentils 99
yellow pea soup 49

Acknowledgements

Recipes: Catherine Atkinson, Pepi Avis, Valerie Barett, Alex Barker, Ghillie Basan, Angela Boggiano, Georgina Campbell, Carole Clements, Trish Davies, Joanna Farrow, Brian Glover, Nicola Graimes, Rosamund Grant, Rebekah Hassan, Shehzad Husain, Christine Ingram, Manisha Kanani, Soheila Kimberley, Lucy Knox, Jane Milton, Keith Richardson, Marlena Spieler, Biddy White Lennon, Kate Whiteman, Elizabeth Wolf-Cohen, Jeni Wright.
Home economists: Angela Boggiano, Annabel Ford, Silvano Franco, Kate Jay, Jill Jones, Emma Macintosh, Lucy Mckelvie, Jennie Shapter, Linda Tubby, Suni Vijayakar, Jenny White.
Stylists: Shannon Beare, Penny Markham, Marion McLornan, Helen Trent.
Photographers: Frank Adam, David Armstrong, Caroline Barty, Martin Brigdale, Nicki Dowey, Gus Filgate, Amanda Heywood, Ferguson Hill, Janine Hosegood, David Jordan, Sara Lewis, Clare Lewis, William Lingwood, Thomas Odulate, Craig Robertson, Simon Smith.